JOLIET PRISON
BLUES

JOLIET PRISON BLUES

BLUES

A CENTURY OF STORIES

AMY KINZER STEIDINGER

THE
History
PRESS

Published by The History Press
Charleston, SC
www.historypress.com

First published 2021

Manufactured in the United States

ISBN 9781467147354

Library of Congress Control Number: 2021931018

To my very supportive and encouraging husband, Jay;
my mom, Denise, who has always been my greatest cheerleader;
and my children, who have grown up to be amazing adults.

CONTENTS

PREFACE

My first book, *So Many Fragile Things*, told the story of Samuel Moser, who was sentenced to the Illinois State Penitentiary at Joliet in 1901. He died there in 1910, shortly before he was to be released. I had done some research and become fascinated with the history of the old prison on Collins Street. In the fall of 2019, my brother and I heard that they'd opened the prison for tours. We ordered tickets and planned a day trip.

We stood in the parking lot with the other tourists who were arriving and gazed up at the imposing walls. Pictures don't prepare you. I imagined Sam being brought here, facing years inside those limestone walls. Then I thought about how many thousands of other stories this building represented. The historian in me was imagining the time periods—Civil War, turn of the twentieth century, Prohibition, Depression era, the world wars, Vietnam. Then a lookalike of the Blues Brothers' mobile pulled up (with the loudspeaker strapped to the roof, even) and I was completely hooked—I just wanted to hear every single story.

Old Joliet Prison: When Convicts Wore Stripes tells the stories of the Old Joliet Prison from 1858 until 1913, when Warden M. Allen brought reform policies. This book picks up at that pivotal moment of change and continues through the closing of the prison in 2002.

ACKNOWLEDGEMENTS

T hanks to the reporters who originally told these stories and took us along on their visits to the prison.

To Heather Bigeck and the Joliet Area Historical Museum for help and encouragement in the completion of this project. For more information, visit jolietmuseum.org.

Thanks to Sandy Vasko and the Will County Historical Society and Research Center just a few short miles north in Lockport, Illinois. For more information, visit willhistory.org.

To Ben Gibson at The History Press, who was such an encouragement through the steps of the process.

To the many historical and genealogical society volunteers everywhere who lovingly tend to the records.

And thanks to my brother, Adam, for beginning this journey with me and sharing a love of things historical—and for the wonderful pictures he took that are included in the books.

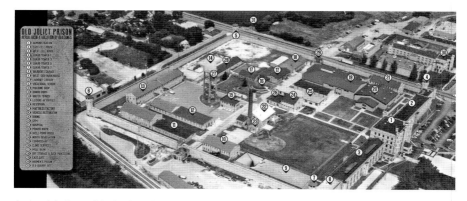

An aerial view with the locations of the buildings. *Joliet Area Historical Museum, Illinois.*

INTRODUCTION

The stories in *Joliet Prison Blues: A Century of Stories* are taken directly from online newspapers unless otherwise noted. Though they were blended, abbreviated, reworded for clarity and greatly simplified, efforts were made to retain the language of the day. The result is very brief mentions of complicated true crime stories. My intention is to give the reader what I wished for on the prison tour—a quick glimpse of lots of different people who lived and worked in the old prison. The reader is encouraged to further research stories of interest—many of them could be a book by themselves.

For all the riots, lockdowns and escapes Joliet has seen, it also has taken its place in American prison history. From the filming of The Blues Brothers *to the unlikely escape of bank robber George "Baby Face" Nelson out of the parking lot, Joliet is not merely a house of correction, but* of *stories. Joliet started the nation's first "honor farm" for model prisoners. Abe Lincoln slept in the warden's quarters (now an administration building) while campaigning for the presidency. In that same building, a warden's wife was murdered in 1915.*

—Lou Carlozo, 2002

1

JOLIET PRISON IN THE NEWS 1900-19

BEHIND THE LIMESTONE WALLS OF JOLIET PRISON

"Look up and hope" was the motto on the little blue and white button which each member of the Volunteer Prison League wore in ten prisons across the United States. Prisons had an inflexible rule that when a visitor or official or guard passes a prisoner, he shall look at the ground.

A look over the massive stone walls of the administration building. *Joliet Area Historical Museum, Illinois.*

Think of this, you who may have found fault with the ex-convict who could not "look you in the face." Think of the years of degradation in the lock step and see if you can criticize the loose, shuffling movement of the feet which anywhere catches the eye of a city detective and marks the man as an ex-convict.

Think what it is, when years and years of such discipline have crushed out almost human semblance in the man, to ask of him that he come out into the glaring day, look every man in the face and prepare to take up the honorable work of the world, which will not let him touch the hem of its garments.

—Maud Ballington Booth, prison reform advocate, 1900

A HARD PLACE TO DO TIME

A news article from 1902 explained that the very first thing done on the arrival of a convict at Joliet was to impress on him the fact of his utter helplessness. They learned the lesson, because failure to do so was followed so swiftly by retribution that there was no possible escape.

The regulations on the daily conduct of the prisoner were printed on heavy cardboard and hung in each cell. They warned him against speaking in line, looking up at his work, disobeying a keeper, failing to do his task, defacing his cell and being noisy in the cellhouse. There were also many unwritten rules of behavior that he was supposed to learn from his cellmate. Tickets earned penalties—the withholding of the ration of tobacco or of privileges, letter writing once in six weeks or receiving visitors once in four.

The deputy warden was the king inside the walls—his word was law. The warden was the executive, his deputy the administrative officer of the prison. Under his absolute orders were fifty to sixty uniformed officers working under an assistant deputy and a night and day captain, who were known as keepers. Guards carried a wooden baton, which was to be used in self-defense.

The most severe punishment was incarceration in the "hole," a dreaded thing in Joliet. The convict's hands were pressed through the iron bars on a level with his chin and locked there with shackles and the wooden door was closed, and in that intense darkness, he stood hour after hour. He was given bread and water, and for a few hours of the night, he was permitted to stretch out his strained limbs on the bare floor. Occasionally, the doctor looked in and felt his pulse. To most prisoners, one experience of this was enough.

Left: The original cells of Old Joliet Prison were seven feet deep by four feet wide by seven feet high. *Joliet Area Historical Museum, Illinois.*

Right: "These men are serving life sentences. Reading from left to right they have served respectively twenty, eighteen, and twenty-two years and are now sixty, seventy-one and sixty-nine years of age. *From the* Joliet Prison Post *1, no. 3 (March 1, 1914).*

THE YEARS OF REFORM

When Edmund M. Allen took over as warden of Joliet Prison, his policies for humanizing prison administration attracted widespread attention. He ordered that convicts be permitted to converse with one another—an unheard-of thing. "It is the silent man who conspires," he explained. "Force a man into moodiness by refusing to permit him to talk to his fellows and he will occupy his mind plotting. Give him a chance to air his views among his fellow prisoners, and he will feel contented when he gets through. Kicking is a great American privilege, and a convict feels like a human being when he has a chance to indulge in it to his heart's content."

Allen knew all about prison life; his father, Robert L. Allen, was warden of the prison when he was young. There were "lifers" in Joliet who recalled the youngster in knickerbockers. Some of the trustees still called him Eddie. The banishment of the "silence rule" was only one of several changes Warden Allen made in his uplift policy at Joliet.

Prison stripes were abolished, and solid prison gray substituted, followed by denim blues. Only escaped convicts who had returned and those who violated their paroles were distinguished by clothing from the others. They alone still wore the crossbar suits of black and white.

WARDEN EDMUND M. ALLEN TAKES UP THE REINS

Edmund "Ned" McDougall Allen was born in Joliet, Illinois, on February 24, 1871. He married Isabel Fleming in 1894, and they had two children: John Fleming Allen, born in 1896, and Katherine A. Allen, born in 1897. Isabel Fleming Allen died on May 17, 1903, at the age of thirty-three.

Ned was the police magistrate of Joliet when his engagement to Odette Maizee Bordeaux was announced in April 1909. As a widower with two small children, Ned had met the twenty-eight-year-old actress while in New York attending a conference on prisons. She was "a woman of unusual beauty and social and intellectual charms." Said to be originally from New Orleans, Odette had come to Elmira, New York, in 1904. She was a comic opera/vaudeville singer and dancer at the popular Rorick's Glen Theater. A news article said that all of Joliet was "looking forward with great interest" to the wedding in the coming week. They were married on April 22, 1909, in Crown Point, Indiana.

Opposite: The Joliet Prison Honor Band. First organized under the direction of J.F. Saville and later led by bandmaster Guido Mattei. Joliet Prison Post *1, no. 11 (November 1, 1914)*.

Above: Joliet Penitentiary, September 6, 1913. "Mrs. Easterberg, Margaret Easterberg, Wn. E.A.A. Miss Minnie Lind and friends."

In 1913, Edmund Allen resigned as mayor to accept an appointment from Governor Dunne to be warden at Joliet. Newspapers said that the new warden was "highly educated and wealthy." In this sense, he was different from previous wardens, and his ideas were much more progressive than most at the time. Once the appointment was made official, Ned and Odette moved their little family into the warden's quarters inside the state penitentiary. The new warden addressed the prisoners during a chapel service. He spoke of his desire to do the right thing by each man and discussed matters of discipline.

He expressed his policy as one that would make citizens of unfortunate men rather than one of punishment. The convicts welcomed their new warden with a letter, done by hand in old English type and framed. The statement of the convicts read:

> *Congratulations and best wishes to warden Edmund M. Allen. We are happy to greet you as our warden. It recalls in mind the same honor that was conferred upon your father twenty years ago. Many of us retain pleasant recollections of the wise and kindly manner in which he governed his unfortunate wards during the period of his administration. With the precedent established by so grand and noble a father to guide you, we feel confident that our welfare has been entrusted to one whose wisdom and understanding will service our interests not only as prisoners, but as future citizens. Therefore, we most courteously tender you our congratulations and best wishes. Sincerely yours, Inmates of Illinois State Prison.*

Reform measures began when Edmund M. Allen established the honor system at Joliet, which allowed inmates to be rewarded with privileges and better job assignments for good behavior. Inmates were graded on their conduct. The warden understood that before he'd be able to change behaviors, procedures and programs, he'd first have to change minds and hearts. The inmates were given recreation time and allowed to get out and get some fresh air and sunshine. The warden even put together an honor band to play for the inmates during various activities. A day school was begun, and prisoners were given time off of work to study.

EVELYN ARTHUR SEE

Edmund Allen formally assumed the wardenship of the Illinois State Penitentiary at eleven o'clock on the morning of April 26, 1913. Warden Allen, laughing and joking with his companions as he entered the prison as its chief executive, did not notice the white-faced, trembling prisoner who preceded him down the stone corridor.

Evelyn Arthur See, the convicted author of a religious cult embracing the doctrine of free love, who was arrested the year before in a Chicago apartment "temple" where he lived with several unmarried Chicago girls, made his formal entrance into the state prison at the same time that morning. The disciple of "Absolute Life" and high priest of the Chicago "temple" was now convict no. 2928 in the Illinois State Penitentiary. He was a convict until October 1916, when he was released.

> *There is some good in every man…and there exists some influence which*
> *will appeal to his heart and reason.*
> —*Warden Edmund M. Allen, 1913*

THE SLEEP MURDERS

On Monday April 14, 1913, Maud Sleep took her two smallest children out for a walk. She asked her eleven-year-old daughter, Ida, to get supper ready. But dusk came, and Sleep did not return. When Ida's father came in from milking, he and Ida went out to search, hollering for Maud and the children. There was no answer. They asked neighbors to help. An older daughter, Hattie, came from her job at the Elgin watch factory and joined the hunt, which spread throughout the neighboring countryside in the following days. Saturday, the bodies of the mother and her babes were found in the cistern of the house. Near the bodies lay a pistol with four bullets loaded and one empty chamber. There was a note indicating that Mrs. Sleep had killed herself, but it wasn't credible. Mr. Sleep said that the childish handwriting was not his wife's. Investigators revealed that the heavy lid that covered the dry well could not have been manipulated by the woman, even if she hadn't been shot four times in the chest and neck. The children were horribly beaten. In the woodshed were two heavy axes, one of them with what appeared to be blood.

Witnesses were detained on the farm, including two boys who had been paroled from the St. Charles Home for Boys about six months before. They had been sent to work on the Sleep Farm, where they would earn their keep while learning responsibility. Herman Coppes, who was just fourteen years old, was taken into custody and held at the jail in Geneva. He had been arrested some two years before for stealing $2.67 from a schoolteacher.

He had an empty cartridge in his pocket on Thursday and had told another boy that he thought he'd better throw it away or it would get him into trouble. Ida Sleep told police that Herman had displayed a revolver the Friday before while at school that looked like the one found at the bottom of the cistern. She also remembered a time two months before when Herman was chastised by her father. Herman told Ida, "I'll wipe out the whole family someday." Samples of the boy's handwriting were collected.

On Sunday, police went into Coppes's cell and began to question him. At first, he would only admit that he had written the suicide note that was found in the Sleep house. Then, Coppes admitted that he had killed the woman and her babies. Later that afternoon, he was taken from the county jail in Geneva to the scene of the murder. Nearly three hundred "morbidly curious" neighbors and friends of the Sleeps had gathered at the farm to look over the scene of the tragedy. They stood silent as the youth walked through their ranks and entered the kitchen of the little home.

"She told me to do my chores," Coppes said. "I told her I wouldn't do them. She said she would see about it. I shot at her six times. Then I went for an axe in the woodshed and killed the two kids, who were yelling. I raised the trapdoor in the kitchen and dropped all three of them into the cistern."

He couldn't explain the sudden impulse. He'd found the old revolver in a cupboard a few days before and kept it in his pocket. "Mr. Sleep asked me where his woman was, and I told him she had taken the children out for a little walk around the farm. We had supper then. It's a good thing Ida went out to call the old man." From Monday until Saturday, Coppes had eaten his meals at the table directly over the cistern, with no remorse or concern for what he had done.

The newspapers dubbed him the world's first Jekyll-Hyde boy. People just simply could not believe that a fourteen-year-old child could be guilty of this. On June 2, the judge imposed the sentence of life imprisonment on fourteen-year-old Herman Coppes. He would be the youngest life prisoner who had ever entered the state prison. He was also the youngest male prisoner, though there were a few girls who were younger. The boy was assigned convict no. 3008 and was put through the regular routine for prisoners received at the prison. He was photographed and measured, given a bath and his first shave and then presented with what was his first pair of long trousers—the regulation gray uniform that convicts wore.

Coppes, who had been chatty and talkative the entire trip to the prison, was gently and firmly told to stop talking when he attempted to speak to one of the visitors who had stopped to look at the youthful convict. He was informed of the rules of the prison and led to his cell. Warden Allen assigned him to the care of the prison chaplain, hoping it would be a good influence.

But by August 2, it seemed that the honeymoon period was over. Warden Allen expressed that Herman Coppes was "the most baffling study in juvenile criminology that has ever come to my notice." Alienists, criminologists and penitentiary officials examined him. Some said that the boy should be sent to an institution for the insane for treatment. They

Pen picture of the career of the young murderer Herman Coppes. *Pittsburgh Press, February 11, 1916.*

admitted, however, that to be treated in such an institution, some freedom would have to be given him. Though he appeared sane, it was felt that he could at any time transform into the boy who killed Mrs. Sleep and her children. Penitentiary officials admitted frankly that they hadn't the slightest idea what to do with the boy.

He had to be watched constantly, especially on mornings when he woke up with a sullen, gloomy look on his face. "A visitor of the warden's brought a dog into the latter's office a few days ago," said one of the guards. "The boy stopped to pat it on the head. When he looked up there were tears in his eyes, and he sobbed openly as he went back into his cell. For the next three or four days he wouldn't leave his cell and we had to make him eat what we took to him."

In October, it was announced that a school for convicts had been organized by the chaplain. Any convict who expressed a desire to attend was excused from other employment. The youngest pupil was Herman Coppes. By the next fall, in September 1914, Herman was reportedly employed in the electrical department of the institution. He had shown a disposition to take up employment at which he would be learning something constantly.

Warden Allen commented that "the boy is one of the problems of the institution. He is full blooded, although in mentality he is behind what he should be for one of his years. He seems to show a good interest in his duties, and he promises to make good."

On August 17, 1924, Herman Coppes (who was then twenty-four years old) was working on an honor farm outside the prison. He and another trustee stole a guard's vehicle and were gone. Warden J.L. Whitman of the Joliet Prison sent a telegram to the detective bureau in Chicago to watch for them. Herman Coppes would be found, but it wouldn't be for many, many years, and it was many miles away.

In June 1944, law enforcement received a request to arrest Albert Huth. The man had lived in Denver for eighteen years, working the last three years on naval vessels. Authorities claimed he had escaped from Joliet, where he was serving a term for murder—as Herman Coppes.

Huth at first denied this, but when confronted with evidence, he admitted his identity and told of his escape: "After I was in the big house for a long time, they made me a trustee. So one day I was working on the lawns outside and just decided to leave." He had worked odd jobs in Iowa, Nebraska and Denver. In 1929, he married Mollie Kell, who was just eighteen years old at the time. They had six children: Clara was fourteen, Ruth thirteen, William twelve, Richard eleven, Edward six and Raymond two.

He had even been in jail without anyone, including his wife, discovering his past. On May 19, 1934, there was a newspaper story from Denver, Colorado: "The law to which he gave himself up yesterday did not penalize Albert W. Huth, 34, as he expected. It turned him loose to find a job. He surrendered to authorities after a jail break-out January 1930, while he was on a federal charge of operating a whiskey still. On May 23, 1943, he was accused of beating his oldest daughter, Clara, but charges were dismissed."

Huth's wife, Mollie, was shocked when told of the Illinois case but had no sympathy. A divorce action was being prepared, which alleged physical cruelty. Despite his arrests, there was no suspicion of Huth's identity until Warden Joseph E. Ragen of Joliet Prison wired Denver police that Coppes was an escaped convict and sent a fingerprint classification that was matched with Coppes's prints.

He would be returned to Illinois to complete a life sentence. He told authorities that he would do his talking when he got back to Joliet. But he didn't. Whether he decided not to talk, or prison officials didn't want him talking, nothing else was reported. Herman Coppes doesn't appear in the newspaper again until November 24, 1944.

A band of ten prisoners led by Roger Touhy attempted to storm the wall of Stateville Prison. They overpowered a guard and tied him up. Crossing the prison yard, they concealed a ladder between them, taking a guard along as a hostage. A seventy-two-year-old guard in a tower opened fire on the convicts as they started to scale the wall. He was able to shoot four of the convicts and send the others running. However, he also hit the guard, Zoethe Skaggs. The father of four children died two hours later in the prison hospital. Other prisoners involved in the escape were James McDonald, Walter Ferguson, Paul Jenkot and Herman Coppes.

In 1946, Coppes was discharged to the psychiatric division. Fourteen years later, in November 1960, he was ordered paroled. He was released to the home of his nephew Jack on December 9, 1960. Four years later, it was noted on his prison record that his parole period was complete. According to the Social Security Death Index, Herman Donald Coppes died in June 1978 in Denver, Colorado.

THE BLACK HOLLOW MURDERS

On May 27, 1913, Joseph Scuitto, with two other men, held up Ben Dierks, the paymaster of the Black Hollow Zinc mines, near LaSalle, Illinois. They shot the paymaster dead, robbed him of $8,000 and threw his body into a gully. Another man's wounds were so severe that death followed a few hours later at St. Mary's Hospital. Two others were slightly wounded—F.D. Richmond, a civil engineer for Illinois Zinc Co., and Henry Osterle. Ten men and two women were jailed in Ottawa, La Salle and Peru, pending investigation.

At the trial of the Black Hollow murders, which was held in Ottawa in March 1914, the most intense public disgust was expressed with the result of the trial, which gave Scuitto twenty-four years and Gardinni fourteen years in the penitentiary. "Sell the courthouse and throw open the jail," was remarked on the streets following the verdict. Threats were made against members of the jury, who "seemed to hold human life so lightly." They did not stay in the county seat longer than necessary.

PACKEY McFARLAND

July 4, 1913, was a day of rest for the convicts at the Joliet Penitentiary. They were given an exhibition on the finer points of self-defense by Packey McFarland, Chicago lightweight, who made the trip to Joliet for the express purpose of entertaining the convicts with the boxing exhibition. In former years, the convicts staged boxing bouts among themselves, but this was dispensed with this year when it was announced that McFarland was to give an exhibition. After eating breakfast, the prisoners were allowed the freedom of the yard to mingle with each other and talk to their hearts' content.

At eleven o'clock, the prisoners were marched to the dining room. After lunch, they tried something new—ice cream cones. The prisoners were then marched back to their cells and given cigars—all they cared to smoke. They were also allowed to write letters to their folks, Warden Allen making the Fourth a special letter-writing day. The prisoners availed themselves of the favor granted, and almost every man who had relatives awaiting word took this opportunity of telling of the special favors granted on Independence Day by the new warden.

BASEBALL BEHIND THE WALLS

Baseball was one of the innovations that attracted the most attention among visitors to Joliet. Each of the twelve departments of the prison had a team, and there were twelve of them in the league. The baseball diamond was laid out inside the walls, and one hour each day was devoted to the sport. Convicts who were not baseball fans were permitted to spend the time wrestling or boxing. There was nothing to curb the rooting of the fans but the high walls and a rigid rule against profanity, and when two teams met, the comments of the convict fans could be heard for blocks.

Warden Allen umpired most of the games himself. He was probably the least disputed umpire in the world. A new diamond was later constructed outside the walls for the trustees. Warden Allen also adopted the policy of spending so much time every day going about the prison shops and factories, where he mingled with the men. The convicts came to look on him as a friend and advisor. If they felt they had "a grouch or a kick" regarding their life in the prison, he courted criticism from them direct.

"Members of the prison baseball team pose for a team picture. By the 1920s, intramural baseball was a normal feature of inmate life in prisons across the country. Selected players, like these Joliet inmates, manned institutional teams that played against other prison teams as well as against visiting minor league clubs." *Abraham Lincoln Presidential Library & Museum.*

"We are not conducting a pleasure resort here, by any means," said the warden. "Joliet prison is a place where men are incarcerated as punishment for crimes against society. With punishment we strive to mete out to every man confined here a modicum of human kindness, and if possible, turn him away from the pit into which he has fallen and start him right. We are not forgetting for a minute that these men are human beings. We are treating them as such."

FEDERAL CONVICTS

An announcement was made by the federal district attorney in Chicago that all persons sentenced in the federal courts of that city for an indefinite period would be sent to the Joliet penitentiary instead of Leavenworth. Joliet was more convenient to Chicago, and the federal prison was crowded. Women would be sent to the federal prison at Lansing, Michigan.

PLANNING THE NEW PRISON

On August 7, 1913, there was a joint meeting of the members of the Penitentiary Site commission. Plans for the use of the new site for the prospective new penitentiary were discussed. Governor Dunne announced that his administration policy would not include the immediate erection of the new prison on the site; it was decided to use the ground the next year as a state penitentiary farm. Plans were made for the erection of two new buildings for the housing of tools and agricultural implements and arrangements for the superintendence of the new state farm.

INTERNATIONAL CONFIDENCE MAN

On August 21, 1913, Jeff Sharum escaped. A reward of $200 was offered for the noted forger, who was fifty-five years old at the time. He'd first been tried and convicted of murder in April 1883 but was pardoned in August 1885. From that time on, there was hardly a year in which his record did not appear in the archives of the Department of Justice in Washington.

He was brought back to Joliet and continued on until August 1915, when President Wilson took a year off of his sentence. Sharum was said to be old and had helped the Secret Service capture a lot of paper that had been used for counterfeiting. He was then sent to Texas, where he was wanted on charges of forging money orders.

When he was due to be released in 1916, he was wanted in both Massachusetts and Indiana. The newspaper noted that "virtually his lifetime has been spent in different prisons for forging checks and money orders." In 1923, he was named as the dominant figure in a $40,000 racetrack swindle in New York City. (He was captured in New Orleans.) He was sentenced to serve five years in Atlanta. In 1932, he was arrested with seven others in "a far-reaching stock and race swindle racket being worked to fleece winter visitors out of thousands of dollars" in Florida. Having also done time in England, "Little Jeff" was said to be an "international confidence man."

In 1935, Jeff was on his way to Reading, Pennsylvania, to answer charges on a $14,000 swindle. He was then seventy-eight years old. In 1938, he was in court in Crown Point, Indiana, where the court revealed the record of Sharum's sentences all over the country. The man had been sentenced to jail in "every State in the Union, except Maine." Sharum defended himself, saying that he never "took" an honest man—he had confined his activities to "taking in suckers." He never felt sorry for them because they were "trying to get something for nothing." The eighty-year-old man's hair was silver. His eyes were still twinkling, and his face bore the same kindly expression that "took in" many a sucker from coast to coast.

HENRY SPENCER

In September 1913, Henry Spencer confessed to twenty-five murders. He told detectives that he was the arch-murderer of history, that he was a lover of death. He killed to avenge himself against society because of mistreatment he underwent at the hands of almost everyone who knew him when he was a boy. "There's only one thing coming to me," he said almost cheerfully, making a gesture toward his neck. "That's the rope." He sent a cloud of cigar smoke into the air and said, "And I don't care how soon."

By early October, it was clear that Henry Spencer's confessions were fiction, woven by an opium-clouded brain. He continued to relate fantastic stories of crimes, but he could not have committed most of them because he was in prison at the time.

Guards at the penitentiary remembered Spencer well, although not by the name Spencer. He was known as Skarupa to them. He had been employed about the prison yards at odd jobs during his previous imprisonment.

Spencer claimed that he trailed E.J. Murphy, former warden of the Illinois State Penitentiary, for over two years and planned to kill him, following alleged ill treatment received while he was a prisoner at the Joliet Prison. He was most bitter toward ex-warden Murphy and blamed his late criminal actions on the treatment he had received at the prison, especially while confined in the solitary cells.

GEORGIANA DOOLITTLE, ASSISTANT MATRON OF THE WOMEN'S PRISON

Also in September 1913, Warden Allen had the disagreeable duty of discharging one of the prison's most faithful servants. Georgiana Doolittle had been appointed assistant matron in the women's part of the prison by his father seventeen years earlier and held her position through every administration since. Her dismissal was not caused by any infraction of the rules, according to Warden Allen, but because the position was abolished. Her position would be filled in the future by a graduate nurse, who was to be appointed by the Civil Service commission. According to the warden, there had long been the need of a nurse at the prison. The assistant matron's position was done away with so that a nurse could be installed. The nurse would also perform the duties of the assistant matron besides her regular duties, thereby giving the women prisoners more and better attention than they had been receiving.

EX-WARDEN MAJOR MCCLAUGHRY

Major R.W. McClaughry was warden of Joliet penitentiary for fourteen years. He had afterward been the warden at Leavenworth Federal Prison in Kansas, until he retired on July 1, 1913. He and his wife visited Joliet during their first retirement trip. On October 2, 1913, he told reporters, "Joliet gave me some of the happiest days of my life, and I always cherish the fondest recollections of the dear old town and its people. I have not had the pleasure of being here for the past twelve years, but I fear that I will be tempted to come often now that I am free from all responsibilities." Major McClaughry was prominently identified with prison reform since the time of his wardenship at Joliet and was always heartily in favor of any measure that would help to make the convict's life more pleasant. When asked his opinion of the honor system being enforced in the state of Illinois, the former warden replied, "I think it is one of the greatest things that has ever been done for the betterment of social conditions in general, and Governor Dunne is trying out a theory that will in my opinion prove a great boon to the prison annals of the state of Illinois."

AN EXEMPLARY LIFE

On October 4, 1913, Ida G. Leegson was lured by a telephone call to the prairie southwest of Chicago and strangled with a silken cord. Ida was a graduate of the University of Chicago and a student at the art institute. After her identification, little was found to indicate a motive for the crime. Investigation showed that she led an exemplary life, had no men callers at any of the places where she had resided and was not thought to have possessed any large amount of money. Witnesses testified that she had been met by a man. The day after her body was found, a man answering their description entered a pawn shop on the South Side and pawned a watch that was proven to belong to the slain woman. On July 20, 1914, Isaac Bond was found guilty of murdering her and sentenced to life imprisonment by a jury.

POLICEWOMEN

In October 1913, a resolution was passed that two policewomen be appointed to the local force, following the plans of the police departments in other cities. The next morning, Chief of Police Martin Murphy was asked by a representative of the *Chicago Herald* whether there was any necessity for having women police. "No." was the emphatic answer. "What would I do with women on the department?" asked the chief. "There is not enough work here for women to do—in fact, I don't see where we could use them in this city. If they wish to have policewomen in this city, why doesn't the board of education appoint a number of them. The only trouble we have with juveniles comes from that department and possibly a few women could be used to advantage there. Don't misunderstand me now," continued the chief, "I don't mean to say that women would not make good police officers, but we have no work in this city which we could place them at."

THE MILLIONAIRE KID

Edward Morris was sentenced from Kankakee for horse stealing in 1896. He had already been pardoned once, but after breaking his parole and serving a sentence in the Michigan State Penitentiary, he was returned to Joliet to serve out his sentence. According to the prison authorities, Morris was "feebleminded" and for this reason had never been put to work in any of the shops. He was used as a trustee and during the summer had been allowed to work on the farm.

He was called the "Millionaire Kid" by his fellow inmates because he imagined that he inherited a fortune every day in the week. He took great pleasure in distributing the money to his unfortunate fellow convicts. For example, he offered to pay another inmate $20,000 for a bite of chewing tobacco. The other inmates thought this greatly entertaining and encouraged the jest. He had been granted a parole by the state board of pardons at the last meeting but was not told, as officials thought he would not understand. Ten days before he was to be paroled, Edward Morris succeeded in making his escape from the prison farm on October 22, 1913.

A SCENE IN THE COURTROOM

Jerry O'Connor was the leader of a notorious gang of Chicago highwaymen. He had previously been part of a group that beat a guard senseless in an attempted escape from prison. When he was sentenced to life imprisonment in 1912, he waved his arms at the jurors in the box and cried, "I wish I had a gun and some bullets. I'd shoot every one of you."

But when he entered the prison, he seemed to have a change of heart. He worked hard and behaved in order to be made a trustee. He was placed at work in the greenhouse. It was situated outside of the prison walls, and the convict was practically alone most of the night. On December 2, 1913, Jerry O'Connor escaped from the Illinois State Penitentiary. When he failed to show up for his midnight dinner or report to the guard, a search was started for him. No trace of him could be found. The alarm was sounded, and guards were sent to scour the immediate neighborhood.

JOLIET PRISON POST WILL BE CITY'S NEWEST PAPER

On New Year's Day 1914, the first issue of the *Joliet Prison Post* was printed. The monthly issue was considered a great step forward by prison reform experts and welfare workers. The editor and staff were inmates, and its contributors were largely convicts. The columns contained matter relevant to prison life, events and happenings. A special office for the magazine was reserved in the main building.

Peter Van Vlissington was selected to be the editor. He had considerable experience in journalism, having served for five years as the editor of the *Chicago Real Estate News* and was a frequent contributor to the Chicago newspapers. He'd been sentenced to Joliet Prison after being convicted of $1.6 million in forgery in November 1908 after it was found that he was tracing mortgage signatures through a glass desktop cover.

While the paper gave the convicts a voice in the prison, it was hoped that it would also model the correct position the prisoners should take in their attitude toward officials. Vlissington said, "I can see no reason why, with the proper amount of safeguarding, the publication cannot become popular both with the men and with the officials." The first edition opened with the following: "The prisoner who looks for sympathy in this paper, will be disappointed. We hope that he who recognizes his own shortcomings will find encouragement in every number."

A letter of commendation from Governor Dunne on the plan of issuing the paper was published, along with several articles, discussions

of prison problems, stories, jokes, poems and letters written by prisoners. One interesting feature was the publishing of the Constitution of the United States, which the editor hoped the inmates would peruse. It would be followed by the state constitution, the state laws and the fundamental principles of criminal jurisprudence, which affected them.

Much of the forty-eight-page paper was given over to praise of Warden Edmund Allen, the deputy warden, the prison chaplains and the prison physician. A newspaper editorial commented that the very existence of the prison post "marks a

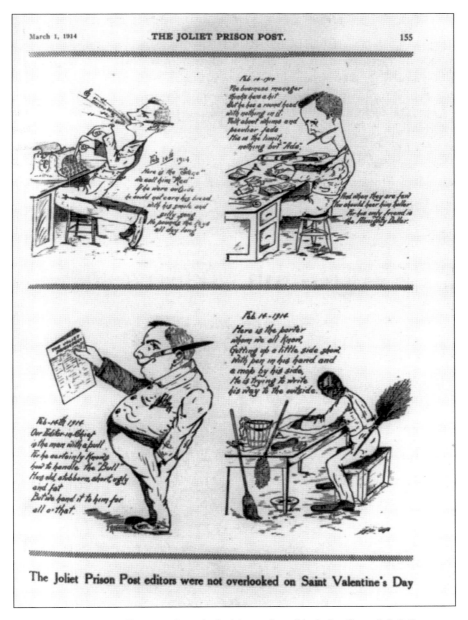

The Joliet Prison Post editors were not overlooked on Saint Valentine's Day

Opposite: Parole law: A life termer begs the legislature for a fair shake. *Cover of the* Joliet Prison Post *1, no. 4 (April 1, 1914)*.

Above: St. Valentine's Day "love letters" honor the *Joliet Prison Post* editors. Joliet Prison Post *1, no. 3 (March 1, 1914)*.

great increase in humanitarianism and enlightened prison management, for it is a startling encroachment upon the old system which regarded a prisoner as a sort of inferior wild animal, only fit to be caged and abused. We shall do much better in our prison administration if we recognize the fact that even prisoners have some rights and that one of them is that they be not regarded as having entirely forfeited their claims to human sympathy and understanding." As a long step in this direction, the establishment of the *Joliet Prison Post* was hailed as a welcome innovation in the penal system of Illinois.

Vlissington was released from prison in July 1916 after editing the *Prison Post* for several years. He planned to seek a position as a foreign war correspondent for an American magazine or newspaper.

FRANK HOLLAND

On March 13, 1914, Frank Holland, a Joliet youth who was in prison for forgery, became violently insane. After clambering to the top of one of the structures, he removed his clothing and prepared to jump off the roof of the chapel. Friendly convicts stopped his plunge.

SILENT FILM

This four-reel, state right, educational picture shows the daily routine of the Illinois penitentiary, known as the "model prison." It emulates the complete interior and exterior workings in every detail. It takes a criminal through his daily life from his incarceration to his discharge. Numberless scenes in the different workshops and the methods adopted in the manufacture of shoes, chairs, brooms, brushes, etc., and the humane manner in which each is conducted is both gratifying and interesting. The scenes in the kitchen and dining room show utmost cleanliness. Simple games are indulged in, such as pitching quoits, etc. Scenes illustrating chapel services and the marches thereto, and to and from their cells show that the old lock step has been relegated to oblivion; also the striped suits are not used, except in extreme cases. Scenes at Mount Hope, where the convicts are allowed to work without guards, are elucidated. This is a very well-made offering.
    —*The* Moving Picture World, *April 11, 1914*

HONOR MEN BEING TRANSFERED TO HONOR FARM, ILLINOIS STATE PENITENTIARY, JOLIET, ILL.

Honor men being transferred to the honor farm. *Joliet Area Historical Museum, Illinois.*

UNDERCOVER AUTHOR

Max Erxleben, twenty-eight, a guard in the Illinois state prison, was making about $70 a month as an overseer on the penitentiary farm. On June 24, 1914, he confessed that he was "Larry Evans," the mysterious author of *Once to Every Man*, a popular best seller, and scores of short stories, which had been published in almost every prominent magazine in the country. Erxleben was making more than $5,000 a year from his writing, which occupied his spare time. He was uneducated and was a former attendant at the Kankakee State Hospital for the Insane. He worked there and in the Joliet Prison merely for information to embody in his writings. He kept his literary identity a secret for five years.

ALL-NIGHT MANHUNT

On July 19, 1914, two of the honor men escaped. Jack Gromo and Joe Smith were among the squad employed in cultivating the new unguarded penitentiary farm in Lockport township a few miles north of the prison. Gromo had received his sentence from Joliet after a wild career that had started when he was a juvenile. He was serving an indeterminate term for highway robbery. Joe Smith had shot and killed a man in Chicago. He was sentenced to a life term in 1910. The two men broke their "honor pledge" to Warden M. Allen and quietly walked away at about ten o'clock on Sunday. For the first time during his administration as executive of the Illinois state penitentiary, Warden Allen personally headed a posse of prison guards in an all-night man hunt. They scoured the country that night and the next morning in search of them with little success. The men at the prison farm felt as bad about the escape as the prison officials. They offered a thirty-five-dollar reward for the return of the men who had violated their pledges. It was presumed that the men were headed for Chicago, where the police were asked to search for them.

A KNIFE FIGHT

In August 1914, James O'Neill, a Chicago burglar serving his third term, got out of the penitentiary with Oscar Van Hagen. Jerry Collins, a guard, fired at them, killing Van Hagen instantly and wounding O'Neill. Despite his wound, O'Neill grappled with the guard and, strengthened by his many years in the quarry, overpowered him and got away. William Carver, another guard, found him at Hackersville, Illinois. Carver was armed with only a pocketknife. O'Neill also had a knife. The men met and fought a duel with their knives in the streets of that village, and O'Neill, though he fought with desperation, was gashed and cut. He fainted from loss of blood and was taken back to prison.

LET HONOR MEN USE DYNAMITE

So satisfied were officials of the Joliet penitentiary that the forty-five "honor convicts" working on the roads of Lee County would do nothing desperate that large quantities of dynamite were distributed among a portion of the workers to blast rocks. The work of cutting down a big hill and improving the ridge road in Grand Detour township was started in September 1914. It was promised to be a model highway, one the state of Illinois could be proud of. The Sunday before they began was a big event at "Camp Hope." A flag was presented by Odette Allen, wife of the warden. Ministers were on hand to conduct services. During the several days before, crowds of curious spectators were refused admittance to the convicts' habitat.

TERROR IN THE STREETS

On October 29, 1914, the *Wilmington Advocate* reported that pedestrians had scattered in terror when thirty-five armed guards pursued two escaped convicts down the principal streets of Joliet, firing a fusillade of shots after them. The men were captured.

BOYHOOD FRIENDS

Frank Repetto, product of Chicago's Little Italy and inmate of the state penitentiary, murdered his boyhood friend and fellow convict in the penitentiary dining room at noon on September 17, 1914. Witnesses testified that Charles Masters was standing peacefully at his table waiting for the signal to sit down when Repetto, who was sitting with his mates at another table, jumped at him, brandishing a knife. "Take him away," shrieked Masters, according to the testimony, and shrank behind another man. Repetto lifted his knife and dug it deep into the other's heart. Repetto was hanged in the Will County jail yard in July 1915.

A LITTLE SUNSHINE

Grace Fuller believed that the debt society owes to its unfortunates should be repaid by giving them every possible opportunity to learn to live under normal conditions. As the superintendent of women at the Illinois State Penitentiary at Joliet, she was putting her theory into practice with the support of Warden Allen and with gratifying results.

On March 20, 1915, a group of white-clad, smiling women stood about their leaders in a domestic science classroom. They beat eggs, measured sugar and whipped batter, all according to the recipes one of them had written on a blackboard. Laughter and talk came easily as they worked. These women were prisoners of the state penitentiary, but they were transformed into new, happy persons by the application of a scheme of revolutionizing prison methods.

Dressmaking, rug weaving and other domestic activities were included in the new rule of procedure for women in this institution. Everywhere was noticeable a sense of contentment and absence of restraint. "It is to give these women, who did not have adequate opportunities before they came

"Miss Grace Fuller instructing women at Joliet Women's Prison, Joliet, Illinois," January 22, 1915. *Courtesy Chicago History Museum.*

here, an opportunity to qualify for normal society that we are doing this work," explained Fuller. "Society should feel that it has placed these women here to help them, not to take its revenge on them. This we are trying to do in giving them work which will fit them, as they leave us, for fine, effective living. Their lives have in so many instances, been barren of all interests before coming here. We ought to supply that interest."

> *Men, more than anything else, cause women to be imprisoned in penal institutions.*
>
> *—Frances Cowley, matron of female convicts, 1914*

ON THE SQUARE

When Deputy Warden William Walsh died on June 8, 1915, inmates mourned his passing by erecting a temporary monument at home plate on the baseball field and suspending play for four days. As Warden Allen's deputy, Walsh had been directly involved in implementing prison reform and establishing the Honor Farm. In an unusual display of affection for a prison administrator, many inmates openly wept when they learned of Walsh's death. The monument they built to honor their "friend" was decorated with flowers and featured Walsh's picture draped in crepe. Beneath the photograph was an inscription that memorialized the deputy warden as "a man who was on the square with us."

—*Robert Sterling,* Joliet Prisons: Images in Time

JAILBREAK INTERRUPTED

On June 13, 1915, two Italians were captured in the main corridor of the penitentiary with a suitcase full of dynamite, revolvers, knives and bombs. They confessed they had arranged to blow up the administration building to free Scuttio, who committed the Black Hollow Murders in 1913.

THE MURDER OF WARDEN EDMUND M. ALLEN'S WIFE

On Saturday, June 19, 1915, Warden Allen and his wife were preparing to leave on a ten-day trip to the hot springs resorts in the French Lick/West Baden area of Indiana. The resort catered to the rich and famous, and the Allens would see and be seen by the social elite. Since Odette's dresses were not yet back from the dressmaker, she decided to wait until the next morning to leave. She encouraged Edmund to proceed without her and went to the movie theater that evening with her two stepchildren. They were driven back to the warden's quarters at 10:45 p.m. by a convict-chauffeured car.

Shortly after six the next morning, guards noticed smoke coming from the warden's quarters. Some guards, along with convicts from the volunteer fire department, managed to break down the door to Odette's bedroom. It took ten minutes to extinguish the flames. When the smoke cleared, it was discovered that the fire had been mainly confined to Odette's bed. There, they found her lifeless body, badly charred. But investigators were able to tell that her skull had been crushed by a blunt instrument. The Allens' physician, who was also a convict, serving time for the murder of his wife, claimed that Odette had been strangled and sexually assaulted. Warden Allen was notified of the tragedy and immediately returned to Joliet. Speechless with grief, he did not go to the penitentiary.

There were about two hundred trustees in the prison at the time, and each had the freedom of the buildings and grounds within the outer walls of the penitentiary. Nine of them were about on that Sunday morning. It was first thought that only one of these had the right to enter the private quarters of the warden. "Chicken Joe" had been a beloved, trusted friend of both Mr. and Mrs. Allen.

Campbell was locked in an isolation cell. He was forced to stand upright, with no sleep and only bread and water. Deputy Warden Ryan and four other prison officials entered his cell at midnight and questioned him for two hours. He said that Odette had rung for him at 6:00 a.m. He carried a thermos bottle up and filled the water container on the nightstand. She asked for coffee and the newspaper, which he delivered. Joe was told to take Mike, her terrier puppy, outside to play. (Witnesses reported that he had come down with the dog at approximately the time given.)

Warden Allen later declared that Campbell's testimony was absurd. "His statements that he took the newspapers to Mrs. Allen at 6 o'clock in the morning are not consistent with Mrs. Allen's habits," said the warden. "She was not an early riser and never bothered about the newspapers until after she had arisen and eaten breakfast." But Campbell had no reason to commit the crime; he was scheduled to appear before a parole board in a little more than a week. Mrs. Allen had agreed to testify on his behalf. (The Allens had previously made three appeals to the pardon board for his release.)

Joe's testimony centered suspicion on Walter Edwards, another Black trustee. He had access to the linen closet, and he was in the building and changed clothes immediately after the fire in a small room near Mrs. Allen's bedroom. A bloody collar belonging to him was found in Mrs. Allen's closet. (He insisted he'd cut his chin while shaving.) Several of the men said that Edwards had told them that Mrs. Allen's body was in bed, when other men in the smoky room could not see it.

But most of the convicts believed Campbell to be the murderer. Their admiration for the warden's wife and their fear that the murder would cost them their honor privileges inspired them with hate. They would rend him to pieces if given the chance.

On Monday, Campbell was called as a witness by the coroner. Campbell was surrounded by twelve guards, who rushed him on the run through the corridors to the jury room. A large number of convicts were in the main dining room over the noon hour, when a man rose from his seat and shouted, "Boys, follow me, and we'll string him up!" A hoarse cry reverberated through the mess hall. Seventeen convicts leaped from their seats and started to gather around the leader. Cursing and hurling chairs, the prisoners started for the corridor leading to the solitary cells, yelling, "Give us Campbell!"

Armed guards seized them and hustled them off to their cells, while other deputies scattered through the room to prevent further trouble. Mutterings and rumblings continued until the warden's brother stood up and announced that he had a message from Warden Allen. In the statement read to the convicts, Warden Allen said, "In this, the greatest trial of my life, I want at least the knowledge that the boys for whom I and mine have tried to do are doing the right thing. I will do nothing until I have talked with you in chapel. If you want to help lighten my grief," Warden Allen told them, "be 100 percent men."

Odette, who was only thirty-four years old, was buried that Tuesday afternoon in the back of Oakwood Cemetery. Most of the city closed down for the funeral. Seven carloads of flowers were left on the grave. She was called the "Angel of the Prison." Newspapers said that the honor system in state prisons had been given a staggering arraignment and declared that the system must go. Warden Allen defended the honor program and begged others not to judge all the men by the actions of one man. On the afternoon of Wednesday, June 23, a letter of sympathy signed by the 1,800 convicts was sent to Warden Allen. It read:

> *At this hour of deepest grief, we send you this message of our love and sympathy. Caesar had his Brutus, Rome its Nero, Jesus the just his Judas, yet the remnants of his disciples remained steadfast and true. Treachery and betrayal were in vain. His work endured. So, in spite of the dreadful blow that has fallen upon us, must the work of yourself and your wife go on. Let us all, you and us, take new hope, and over the grave of her who poured out her love for us join hands and resolve to finish the work which you have begun. The eyes of the world are upon us and we must succeed. We may each and all of us pledge ourselves to wipe out the tragic stain by making your work here a success. The hour has struck and we cannot retreat. Come back to us and we will build together a real honor system as a fitting memorial to your dear departed wife that will be more lasting and enduring than marble or bronze. We will build men in whom honor is not dead and will not die. Our hearts are heavy with grief and our eyes are wet with tears because of this sad tragedy. For your wife and our friend, Odette Allen, words cannot express our thoughts, nor speech contain our love. Signed, Your Boys.*

Edmund M. Allen, warden of Joliet Penitentiary, September 1914. *Chicago History Museum.*

Ten days after the murder, on June 25, the *Herald News* reported, "(Campbell) must prove himself innocent, and the state must prove him guilty. And neither can ever do either. The death is full of mystery, possibly one of the biggest mysteries that state authorities have ever faced." It was reported that Warden Allen wanted to meet personally with each of the eleven men who could have possibly committed the murder. He wanted to ask each man face to face, "Did you kill my wife?" The warden was quoted as saying, "The man who killed my wife must die, but I must be sure that I have the right man. If it is true that the crime was committed by a trustee, then I must admit that the honor system is a failure and that my faith in men is undermined."

Later that month, Mrs. Robert Allen, the warden's mother, took her two grandchildren, Katherine and Jack, and moved to an apartment on Woodlawn Avenue in Chicago. Warden Allen requested that the governor allow him to live outside the prison walls so he would not be reminded constantly of the terrible murder of his young wife. When the request was denied, Allen resigned on August 6. Campbell was convicted on circumstantial evidence and was said to be crushed by the verdict. He was sentenced to death on the hangman's gallows. His sentence was later commuted to life in prison. He died at Joliet Prison in 1950.

BURGLAR GOES BACK TO THE PEN

On August 6, 1915, Roy Williams was arrested for twenty robberies in the city of Alton. He had been paroled from the Joliet Penitentiary, and his parole would have expired in another four months. He agreed to confess if the police would promise that no new case would be made against him. The mayor agreed to these conditions, and Williams assisted in securing a large amount of property that he had stolen. Williams was under the impression that if he was returned to Joliet, he would be allowed to leave at the end of four months. The deputy warden then explained that Williams would have to serve for several years longer for violating his parole.

ELEVEN MEN ESCAPED

Between August 9 and mid-September 1915, eleven men escaped from Joliet. One of these was James Morrison, who was returned on September 23, after he was arrested with two girls who he was training to be crooks. After a "strong-arm" holdup, Frank Miller, who had escaped with him, was still at large.

The Sunday after Warden Allen resigned as head of the penitentiary, three men walked away from the honor farm, and on August 25, three life-term murderers—all from Cook County—escaped in the warden's automobile. The honor farm men were David Anderson, serving life for the murder of Patrick Callahan, a Chicago policeman; Harry Patterson of Vandalia; and E.E. Barlow of Bloomington. "Silent Ed" Smith, Frank Gagen and James Moran were the trio who rode out of the place in the warden's car.

BOOTLEGGING BEHIND BARS

On August 20, 1915, the *Wilmington Advocate* reported that several murders had taken place in the Joliet penitentiary. It was discovered that there was a system of bootlegging in its walls. Another murder took place in late December, when James Perry killed his cellmate, Frank Harrod, with the leg of a chair.

Armed Men Hunt Desperate Trio on Chicago Road

Great excitement was created throughout LaSalle County and adjacent territory in September 1915 by the report that three desperate criminals had escaped from the stone quarry of the Joliet penitentiary. Men with rifles and revolvers were looking for the escapees on every road between Chicago and Joliet. The men were Clarence Brown and James O'Neill, both Chicago burglars, and Joe Scuitto, serving a twenty-five-year sentence for a murder. The men were in stripes—the uniform of disgrace under the honor system. When the men were walking through the gates into the main penitentiary building for supper, the checkers missed the three men. The quarry was searched, but there was no trace of them.

The quarry was shut in with a twelve-foot wooden fence, on which barbed wire was strung. It was believed that the trio climbed this fence. Brown was found in the quarry in the morning. O'Neill and Scuitto were recaptured after a fist fight in the quarry at seven o'clock that night. They were hidden in a hole in a far corner of the quarry and were discovered when members of a posse heard a stone fall in the pit. The men were overpowered and placed in solitary confinement.

Christmas Pardons

On December 14, 1915, it was announced that four murderers then serving time in prison were given commutation of sentence by Governor Dunne "as Christmas presents." Three of them were in for life, and the other was up for fourteen years. All would be released on Christmas Eve. On the list from Joliet was Daniel Driscoll, who was sent up from Cook County in 1899 for life on a charge of murder. He was the driver for the warden's carriage at Joliet Prison for several years and was one of the best-known trustees in Joliet. He killed Robert J. Walsh, a Chicago real estate man, in a quarrel over a dance hall business. Another beneficiary of the Christmas pardons was Mattie B. Smith, a Black woman sent to the women's prison at Joliet in 1910 for fourteen years for the murder of her sweetheart, John Crayton. She was sentenced from Williamson County.

CHIEF OF DETECTIVES

On December 15, 1915, John J. Halpin, former chief of detectives, was found guilty of graft by a jury. Halpin fought the charge that he received $500 protection money from "Barney Bertsche." He supposedly listened to the "squeals" of James and Frank Ryan, the clairvoyants who turned state's evidence to send their former protector to prison. Halpin's wife insisted that he'd never taken a bribe in his twenty years on the police force. Halpin was called the one-time master of the Chicago detective bureau and the most powerful police potentate the city had known in many years. Newspapers said he "looked through the gloom of the courtroom last night and saw the gray walls of Joliet before him." He was convicted of "bribery and conspiracy to defeat the ends of justice."

Almost two years later, on October 15, 1917, a young woman named Dorothy Crosby attempted to leap to her death from the second story of the Bismarck hotel. She alleged that so-called dance rooms like Colosimo's and Freiberg's were places of meeting for rich and immoral young men, where women were the pawns in the game. When the police pulled her from the window ledge, Crosby identified "Judge Adams" (the one who had introduced her to the Bluebird Room) as Joe Bertsche, brother of Barney Bertsche, who was named in the graft investigation that sent John J. Halpin to the penitentiary.

Halpin was released from the state prison on parole on February 1, 1918, having served eleven months of an indeterminate sentence for official corruption. Mr. and Mrs. Halpin left at once for Chicago, where he said he was ready "to begin all over again from the bottom."

FIRE AT JOLIET PRISON

The broom shops at the Illinois penitentiary were destroyed by fire on February 26, 1916. There were two hundred convicts in this department of prison work who would remain idle until they could be filled in other branches. The cause of the fire was unknown.

PINKIE, POLLY AND ALES GO TO PRISON

On March 17, 1916, the *Wilmington Advocate* reported that Joliet Penitentiary had opened its steel arms to receive Benjamin Fein, no. 4770; Harry

Kramer, no. 4771; Charles Kramer, no. 4772; and Alex Brody, no. 4773, the Washington Park national bank robbers, into its unhappy citizenry. Stripped of the spectacular and daring, the four gangsters were marched into the great gray building to serve out their sentences of from one year to life imprisonment. The bravado and the sneering manner of the outlaws, who boasted their allegiance to Gyp the Blood and the New York gangs, were gone. In the atmosphere of cold stone and metal, of furtive whispers and hollow sounds, they became merely four more miserable humans. The "natty" clothes were replaced with the drab prison uniform. The "classy" hair was shorn to the fashion of the prison. They were no longer "Pinkie" and "Polly" and "Ales" but numbers. Later, they were to be assigned to prison work. At the bench, they were to take up the first labor they had done since, as boys, they were led on the false trail of "easy money."

DEATH AND DESTRUCTION

In June 1916, the *Wilmington Advocate* reported that Lincoln Whitney, fifty years old, foreman in the rattan shop of the penitentiary, was struck down by Gen Tate, a Black convict who was angered because Whitney ordered him to work faster. Whitney was felled by a blow from a chair rocker wielded by Tate. Convicts prevented Tate from further attacking the foreman and rushed the man to the solitary cells.

It was reported that Bessie Scott, a woman convict in the Illinois State Prison, might die as the result of burns caused by the explosion of a gas stove in the female prison. She was employed as a waitress in the dining room and roughed a match to an open jet. The explosion threw her across the room. Her clothing was afire when Deputy Warden Peter Klein, aroused by her screams, found her. She was twenty-five years old and serving time for murder.

The parents of Harry Thompson of Chicago called at the penitentiary to see their son, who was a convict. They received word that he was dead, having been killed by coming in contact with a high-tension wire that furnished power to the prison electrical plant. He was cutting grass around the edges of the quarry when he got mixed up with "the wire of death."

A MAN WITH GOOD TASTE

In October 1916, the Osburn Mercantile Co. store was burglarized. Ernest Olis, a convict who had escaped from Joliet Prison, gained entrance through a rear door by breaking the glass and unfastening the inside lock. He inspected the entire Osburn stock and helped himself to the best in the store, two good sets of clothes, underwear, shirts, a hat and ties, and then left his prison garb in exchange. He also got a gold watch, a fob, stickpins and other small articles. He was captured a month later in Bloomington, Illinois.

THE MATINEE THIEF

The *Minneapolis Star Tribune* reported on November 5, 1916, that Mrs. Nellie Hantz, Chicago's "Matinee Thief," just loved to burgle. She operated in the afternoon, as she was afraid of the dark. She would rob houses while the women were out shopping or at the movies. She returned each evening before her husband arrived and kept him in ignorance of her exploits. Police said Hantz had made more than one hundred thefts, obtaining $5,000 in loot. Five detectives entered the modest home of the suspect. The dramatic report in the papers said: "She greeted them with a smile but guessed their mission. Whipping a revolver from her skirts, she raised it and would have fired had not an officer seized her from behind and overpowered her."

Newspaper pen drawing of Nellie Hantz, "She Stole for the Fun of It." *Ford County Press, Melvin, Illinois, January 26, 1917.*

A number of her victims dropped in on her at the Hinman police station to positively identify her as the woman who was seen in their flats. Three of the four recovered some of their stolen property, but Hantz told police she could not remember what became of most of the things she pilfered. It was later found that she had actually thrown many of the items into the river.

Hantz admitted that she was a compulsive thief who stole even though she didn't need the money. The forty-year-old woman had a comfortable home; she'd been married for sixteen years and had a twelve-year-old daughter. She told police she'd been stealing for nine years. "I'd go from house to house sometimes—posing as an agent with something to sell. I'd get in, pretend to be a little faint and ask for a drink of water. I'd be in the front and when the lady would go to the rear, I'd take anything I could see."

In February 1928, Nellie had been arrested nine times, spending ten of her previous twenty years in prison. She told the judge that liquor was responsible for her troubles and begged for another chance, which was refused in view of her past record.

A BOHEMIAN HYPNOTIST

On December 5, 1906, Mrs. Martin Vrzal was found dead, a supposed suicide. She was the sixth member of the family to die under strange circumstances over the previous nine months. Her husband and four children had also fallen after brief illness. Her daughter Emma Neuman went to the police with information, which resulted in the arrest of Professor Herman Billick, a Bohemian hypnotist, clairvoyant and fortuneteller. He was accused of hypnotizing Mrs. Vrzal and her daughters and feeding Mr. Vrzal and sister Mary strange medications. They died soon after. Billik was said to have been with Mrs. Vrzal shortly before she swallowed chloroform, and valuables were missing.

Billick told investigators that all had died from natural causes and that Mrs. Neuman was just a hysterical woman, but the coroner's examination of the bodies revealed traces of arsenic poison. Herman Billick Jr. and Jerry Vrzal, the surviving boy of the family, talked to police, revealing that Mrs. Vrzal once went to Cleveland with the intention of killing Mrs. Billick, the hypnotist's mother, by putting poison into a cake. Mrs. Neuman was the target of another plot. She woke up in the night to find the windows and doors closed and the gas pipes leaking. Billick claimed to be out of town, but it was said that he and Mrs. Vrzal were in a conspiracy to obtain life insurance.

At first, he was found guilty and sentenced to hang. Later, Jerry Vrzal recanted his testimony that he had seen Billick pour poison into his family's coffee. Vrzal said that police had intimated that if Billick were not convicted, Jerry might be accused of the murders. By 1908, the case had been taken all the way to the Supreme Court. Over six hundred prisoners in the jail joined in prayers for Billick's reprieve, and Father O'Callaghan of St. Mary's Catholic Church fought to clear Billick. Finally, in 1909, Governor Charles S. Deneen commuted the sentence to life imprisonment. Billick went to Joliet Prison. Father O'Callaghan continued to fight for Billick's freedom, and finally on January 5, 1917, Billick was pardoned after serving eight years on perjured testimony. It was said that he was given the news while laid up in the prison hospital, where he was recovering from rheumatism contracted while working nights in the prison bakery. The news of freedom brought tears to his eyes.

A reported romance between Billick's nineteen-year-old daughter and Jerry Vrzal captured the public's imagination, though it appeared to be only a rumor. Billick told reporters that he was the "happiest man in the world." His wife had stuck by him, and he was looking forward to pork chops after years of boiled beef at Joliet. The surviving Vrzal sisters, however, were very bitter about the pardon and their brother's role in Billick's release, saying that he was a "bad egg." Billick died only five months later in May 1917.

Two Chair Factories Burned

In January 1917, a disastrous fire caused the loss of two chair factories and menaced the lives of 1,700 inmates of the prison. But for the quick and diligent work of the fire brigade, consisting of convict trustees, and the Joliet fire department, other buildings would have been destroyed.

The 1917 Riot

On June 5, 1917, inmates at the penitentiary were told that the temporary warden was restricting the visiting list to relatives of prisoners only. Tables were overturned and dishes hurled at the guards. The inmates formed in groups and marched about the enclosure. Disorder broke out fully when fire was discovered in the rattan factory. Though the fire was put out, prison firemen who tried to battle the flames were assaulted by convicts.

Deputy Warden Bowen called for the militia. The smoke was dense, and it was feared that under its cover convicts might climb over the walls. It was nearly noon before a sufficient force had arrived to make progress against the outbreak. The troops were given orders to not willfully injure the convicts. After six hours of violence, 200 of the 1,600 convicts remained herded in a corner of the prison wall, fenced in by soldiers with bayonets. They jeered at the soldiers and threw anything they could lay their hands on.

That afternoon, the casualties were reported: one dead and eight injured. John Flaherty, a lifer, was killed by jumping from a window of the burning rattan factory. Two guards were injured, one by a thrown missile and the other by a ricocheted bullet. Three convicts were hurt when clubbed by rifles or prodded by bayonet. Five buildings were damaged in the fires; three were saved, but the paint shop and the chapel were destroyed.

On June 6, prison officials revealed that the revolt was planned with care the night before. A.L. Bowen, acting warden, blamed the "misguided interference of women" in efforts at prison reform. "Two years before, a league interested in welfare work was given permission to work in the penitentiary," he said. "The chief purpose of the organization was to supply women correspondents for the men. The mail became loaded down with letters, some from seventy-year-old women, others from schoolgirls of fourteen and fifteen. Their letters, for the most part, were of the most suggestive character, and a favorite pastime of the prisoners was to gather and read their letters to each other, speculating on the appearance and character of the writers. The revolt had its inception in my order that the letters and personal visits should cease."

H.N. Stokes sent a lengthy denial that letters written by members of his organization had anything to do with the recent mutiny of convicts. "I am astonished at the statements of Acting Warden Bowen," he said. Stokes was formerly the librarian of the Oriental Esoteric League, which conducted research in oriental subjects. The league severed connections with Stokes, and he started an organization called the O.E. Library League, under which name he secured the names and addresses of thousands of unsuspecting spinsters and well-meaning women who he encouraged to write to convicts.

A RETURN TO DISCIPLINE

On June 9, 1917, E.J. Murphy, fourteen years the warden of Joliet, returned to his post after an absence of four years. The old disciplinarian was back on the job, and the honor system, as exemplified for the past four years, was to go. Under Murphy's rule, the "law of silence" was in force. Convicts were not permitted to speak to each other and turned their faces to the walls when visitors toured. "I will not knuckle down to existing conditions," said Mr. Murphy. "I believe each convict is entitled to good food, good clothes, and proper treatment, and I expect work and good behavior in return." Mr. Murphy installed a merit system in place of the honor system.

Unidentified warden, circa 1915. *Joliet Area Historical Museum, Illinois.*

FOUR INJURED IN ATTEMPTED JAIL BREAK

On September 10, 1917, it was reported that outbreaks had resulted in the stabbing of three guards and a prisoner being shot. As the convicts of tier no. 9 were leaving the dining room on Sunday, Herman Wienand inspired some of the other prisoners to break ranks. A guard rushed Wienand to a solitary confinement cell, but he broke away, seized a shovel and attempted to strike the guard, who shot him in the neck. There were approximately fifty rioters, fifteen of whom were ringleaders in the riots two months before. They had been in solitary up to two weeks before, when Warden Murphy restored them to their former status. They were still unruly and inclined to growl at the restrictions on privileges instituted by the new warden in an attempt to restore a discipline that had been sadly demoralized by "too much honor system."

THIRTEEN BREAK OUT OF SOLITARY

On December 2, 1917, thirteen convicts broke through four heavy steel doors and escaped from Joliet Penitentiary. A posse of sixty immediately started in pursuit. The men were in solitary confinement, having caused disturbances the week before in the cellhouses. To escape, they had to break out of their individual cells and then saw through two barred doors and finally through a heavy steel door that led into the solitary from the prison corridor. A guard stationed just inside the steel door was beaten unconscious but not before he had summoned the night captain of the guard with his cries. He, too, was beaten, and the convicts somehow managed to climb the fifteen-foot wall at the east gate. They were fired on by guards with rifles in the two towers nearest the gate, but none were wounded. They fled toward the Illinois and Michigan Canal and were lost in the darkness. All were caught within forty-eight hours, except for Reuben LeFlore, who was finally arrested in Memphis, Tennessee, in 1951.

SAMUEL R. MARSHALL

The murder of Mrs. May Marshall on January 29, 1918, was the climax of an affair between a White waitress and a Black man named Samuel R. Marshall, the police said. She was slain with a length of gas pipe. After an all-day search, Samuel, who had lived with May as her husband until the fall before, was arrested at the Pullman company's plant, where he was employed. He denied all knowledge of the crime. The police had established, however, that May visited him at his room. She left the place at about nine o'clock and started for her residence. Two hours later, Marshall was discovered in his room heating water for the purpose of washing bloodstains from clothing. What appeared to be bloodstains were found on a bunch of keys in his pocket. When Marshall was arrested, he was told that he was wanted as a slacker by the federal authorities. Asked if he wanted his wife notified, he said he did not and wept.

THE LANGFORD BROTHERS

Either Clarence Langford was a clever "framer," as well as a bandit and murderer, or else two men and a woman were serving undeserved prison sentences. "Big Gust" Zeidler and Alex McKeown were convicted of robbing the Tri-City State Bank at Madison, Illinois, on May 16, 1918.

But in December 1919, Langford, who was serving a life term for another crime, took full responsibility for the Madison Bank robbery. Langford had killed seven men by the time he was twenty-eight. Langford said his brother, Claude, was a member of the gang in the Madison job and that there was a third man who could not now be reached. This was thought to mean a notorious crook named Clark, whose body was found shortly after the Madison robbery in the river near St. Louis. His throat had been cut and his pockets weighted with stones.

The three Langford brothers were famous in the underworld. It was while saving his brother, Milford, from the law, that Clarence "fell" for his life sentence. Emil R. Leicht, a pawnbroker from Quincy, Illinois, was beaten to death by Clarence Langford with a section of gas pipe. Landford told the pardon board that Leicht was trying to "gyp" him out of $35,000 worth of stolen liberty bonds, which he was selling to the pawn broker.

Milford was the lookout. He was arrested in Kansas City and brought back to Illinois under heavy guard. Clarence boarded the train at Batavia, Missouri, and shot the sheriff, a detective and a passenger who attempted to interfere. He then dragged his brother off the train to where an automobile was waiting for them. Clarence insisted on remaining behind, thinking that he was fatally wounded. Milford escaped, and Clarence was convicted after he recovered.

Margaret Edwards was the "mystery woman" in the case. She steadfastly refused to divulge her identity. She testified that Zeidler (her lover) and his pal McKeown were in her flat in Chicago when the Madison bank was robbed. She was convicted of perjury and taken to the women's department of Joliet Prison.

2

JOLIET PRISON IN THE NEWS 1920-29

PRISON PUZZLE

When Chicago police captured the "mysterious gangman burglar" on September 4, 1920, they solved a string of Hyde Park burglaries. But they quickly became entangled in a new, more baffling mystery. George Williams had posed as an employee of the gas company while looking over homes he expected to rob. He was captured while leaving the apartment of Roy Hartman at 7219 Ebehard Avenue. A neighbor had called the police, who arrived in time to greet Williams as he stepped out of a window. A search of his person revealed a revolver, a "special police" star and two gold watches.

The police believed that George Williams was a paroled convict from the prison at Joliet. When officials consulted the records, they found three men of that name had been paroled in the last three years. None of them fit the description of the George Williams who was then resting in the Hyde Park jail. According to police, this suspect had been arrested in Chicago in 1915 and was sent to the prison at Joliet for a sentence of one to fourteen years for burglary. During World War I, he was said to have volunteered for service at the Rock Island arsenal and was later paroled.

Prison records showed that there was one George Williams received in 1916 for assault to murder, sentenced one to fourteen years and later paroled. Another George Williams was received a year earlier, sentenced to one to fourteen years for forgery and later paroled. The third George Williams was received in 1916 for a confidence game, given an indeterminate sentence of one to ten years and was released on parole. There was no George Williams received in 1915 or 1916 for burglary. In addition to the several George Williams out on parole and in Chicago jails, there were two or three more of them in the penitentiary, officials said.

The *Des Moines Tribune* joked in the September 18, 1924 edition: "Those two young men who went to the women's prison at Joliet to pick out wives evidently wanted theirs already tamed."

A LONG LIFE OF CRIME

Richard Proctor was just seventeen years of age when he broke into the criminal limelight in Columbus, Ohio. He served three years for burglary and was released on June 28, 1898. It took only eight days for him to get into trouble again. On July 6, 1898, he was arrested in Baltimore—caught red-handed while committing a burglary. A month later, before he could be tried, he escaped. This time, he stayed out of trouble for two months. At least, he was not caught again until October 8, 1898, when he was arrested in Chicago and sentenced to Joliet Prison for burglary. He promptly escaped and was arrested for burglary again ten days later in Red Wing, Minnesota. He was known in that trial as Eddie English. He served his time in the Minnesota state prison and at the expiration of his term was taken back to Joliet to serve the remainder of his sentence in the Illinois prison. He was paroled in January 1910.

He fell in love with a burglar's widow. Her name was Red Nell McCarthy, but she was called "Diamond Nell." To satisfy Red's craving for sparkling gems, English thought out a grandiose scheme to blackmail prominent Chicagoans. On his list of prospective victims were Potter Palmer Jr., Hobart C. Chatfield-Taylor, Molly Netcher Newberry, Kellogg Fairbank and Harold F. McCormick. He didn't get far with it. His first letter was to Dr. D.K. Pearsons, demanding $37,000, with a threat of death. The police ran down English, and he was back in Joliet Prison. He was paroled in May 1914, but every time he got out, he fell into trouble trying to please Red Nell.

In October 1917, he was sent back to Joliet as Ed English, "confidence man" from Chicago. He escaped again on May 23, 1920. English and another prisoner sawed the bars of their cell—brand new bars that were supposed to be sawproof—and escaped.

He went to Omaha in March 1922 and took the name Otto Cole. According to numerous identifications at the police station, he had committed a series of holdups and robberies. In early May, he entered Harry Hahn's pawnshop. While attempting to rob the place, he shot and killed the proprietor. He was finally taken into custody after attempting to shoot officers who came to arrest him.

Otto Cole was now forty-two years old and had only thirty-three months of freedom to his credit in the last twenty-five years. Even those months he'd mostly spend as a fugitive from justice. Burglar, con man, booze runner and murderer, he had seen the inside of many jails and penitentiaries. He served time in Minnesota, Maryland, Ohio, Illinois and elsewhere. He escaped from the Baltimore City Jail and the Joliet Penitentiary, among others. He had been paroled, pardoned and released on "good time," in addition to serving out his sentences. But he never kept out of trouble for long. No sooner was he released from a prison than he immediately went back into crime.

Cole appeared before so many different courts that he had picked up quite a smattering of legal terms and methods. He refused the assistance of the public defender and asked permission of the court to conduct his own defense. This was granted, and throughout the trial, Cole carried on his end of the case like a veteran attorney. "Crookedness don't pay," he told the Omaha court. "I ought to know." He was sentenced to life imprisonment. He announced that he intended to devote himself to the study of mechanical engineering.

On April 11, 1941, the Nebraska parole board announced that he would be released. The sixty-one-year-old was being sent back to Joliet as a fugitive. Someone asked English if he expected to see Red Nell again. "Red Nell?" he said. "I haven't thought about her for fifteen years. Joliet's where I'm going." At sixty-one years old, Eddie English had spent thirty-six years of his life in prison.

FATHER, IN CELL, GETS NEWS OF SON'S DEATH

In his cell at the penitentiary, Thomas Inns received word that his son, Thomas Inns Jr., twenty-one years old, had accidentally killed himself when he rushed in the backyard with his shotgun to drive away chicken thieves. Apparently, the boy stumbled and dropped the gun, which exploded. The discharge passed up through his throat and jaw. The father was received at the prison on June 12, 1917, under a seventeen-year sentence for murder and for wounding a man in a diamond robbery in 1915.

Warren Lincoln

On January 10, 1923, Warren Lincoln murdered his wife, Lina, and her brother Byron Shoup in Aurora, Illinois. The lawyer and horticulturist then burned their bodies in his greenhouse furnace. He disappeared in April after faking his own murder. When he ran out of money, he returned, telling tales of abductions and "dope rings," forced on him by his wife and her brother. He disappeared again in the fall of 1923. When he was caught by police in Chicago on January 12, 1924, he confessed to the crime. Alienists from Elgin Asylum and Mercyville Sanitarium in Aurora, Illinois, examined Lincoln and found him to be sane. His son, John, twenty, was taken in for questioning and was suspected of helping his father with the murder. Although he was cleared, it was found that he knew of the murder and protected his father. When the verdict was read at his father's trial, John threw his arms around him. They both wept with relief that Warren would not hang. He was sentenced to life imprisonment and died behind bars at the age of sixty-two.

"Lawyer, horticulturist, and murderer, Warren J. Lincoln tends his garden in Aurora, Ill. off of Old Indian Trail, circa 1923." Chicago Tribune *historical photo.*

HENRY J. "THE MIDGET" FERNEKES

On December 29, 1921, Henry J. Fernekes robbed the First National Bank of Pearl River, New York. Two bank employees were shot and killed. When police arrested a Chicago crook, he told them that Fernekes was experimenting with a new sort of silent explosive and could be found studying in the John Crerar Library. On April 16, the "lone wolf," Henry Fernekes, was captured there by Pinkerton detectives. At the time of his arrest, he was deeply engrossed in a book on the chemistry of gasses. Three revolvers were found on his person, two of which were equipped with silencers.

At that time, he was suspected in eleven bank robberies in the Chicago area and over fifty in various parts of the country. He was apparently preparing for his next big heist. The plot—described by police as a "monster" bank robbery plot—targeted a bank in Chicago's loop district and involved a small army of men. Police raided a boardinghouse and found weapons, gas, smoke bombs and other accessories, including 335 sticks of dynamite.

"The plans were for Fernekes and at least nine others to come to a loop bank in two big automobiles," said a detective. He continued:

> *They were prepared with pump guns and revolvers enough to equip an army. Also, they had the most modern offensive weapons known to science. There were three big tanks of ammonia, gas masks for themselves and ten big smoke bombs to cut off pursuit. The plot called for the gang to slip into the bank, close all doors and take off the caps from the ammonia tanks. The poison fumes would drive out all persons in the place while the robbers, protected by gas masks, were to gather up bank notes and gold and then leave by the rear entrance. They were ready to shoot it out with police and in a chase, they were to use the smoke bombs to elude their pursuers.*

It was found that his criminal record went to 1914, when he was arrested after he had held up the Phoenix Building Loan Association. Armed with two guns, he staged a "wild west holdup" in an office on the tenth floor, then went into the adjoining office and held up two women employees of a realty company. Before leaving, Fernekes told the two women to sit near a front window so that he could take their picture as a souvenir. He was arrested while adjusting his camera. He became known as the "honeymoon robber" after he told police that he had been married just three months and was forced into a life of crime in order to support his wife. "I found I couldn't make more than $10 a week at honest labor, and with the country full of millionaires who do nothing, I turned bandit, that's all." He was sentenced to two years in the Illinois State Reformatory. His wife got a divorce.

Fernekes was also wanted by the authorities in connection with a series of robberies in Pennsylvania and New York. He was suspected in the murder of two Pennsylvania state policemen in 1921 (when they surprised him while he was robbing a bank); the murder of policeman Edward C. Dollar in Monticello, New Jersey, in September 1923; and holdups of the Inland Trust & Savings bank and the Parkway State Bank of Chicago.

On August 5, 1924, Fernekes was taken to the Illinois State Penitentiary at Joliet, surrounded by double guard, to begin serving his term for robbing the Inland State bank of $4,000. But he was brought back to Chicago in September to face trial on charges of murder in another bank robbery. Fernekes and two companions had blocked the automobile of the treasurer of the Pulaski Building and Loan Association when he was making a delivery to the bank. They stole $11,950, shooting the treasurer when he resisted. During the trial, a bailiff discovered that the heavy iron grating was missing over a transom in the bullpen adjoining the courtroom in which Fernekes and his co-defendants waited. Fernekes was about to climb through the transom to freedom when the bailiff made his discovery. The three men were found guilty on January 22, 1926, and sentenced to hang in the Cook County jail.

A search of Fernekes's cell turned up steel saws, razors, files and a coil of wire. Glyceride powder and dynamite caps were found in the mattress. Fernekes had somehow obtained a wax impression of the keyhole in the gate leading over the bridge of sighs to the Criminal Courts building. He was kept under heavy guard in military confinement to foil plans for his escape before the day set for his execution, February 19. But three days before, petitions for a review of the evidence were granted. Efforts of the prosecutor to get speedy justice, they claimed, had robbed them of a fair trial.

On July 18, a bomb was exploded against an inner wall of the Cook County jail, near the cell of Midget Fernekes. Most of the prisoners were locked in their cells at the time. The only ones in the bullpen—where inmates were released at intervals for exercise—were trustees mopping the floor. Fernekes had been exercising in the jail corridor at the time of the explosion and began to run toward the scene. A guard grabbed him and locked him up.

The explosion tore a hole eighteen inches across and within three inches of penetrating the eight-inch brick wall. It would have taken but a moment's work to push out the remaining bricks. The assistant warden and a dozen guards sprang out to surround the jail. Ten squads of detectives were at the jail within a few minutes. The blast was heard for blocks around the jail. Hundreds of citizens rushed to the scene and remained to gape at the guards, who stood ready with shotguns and orders to shoot to kill any prisoners attempting an escape.

Inside the jail, prisoners who'd been deafened by the explosion were in panicked fear that the roof of the rotting old structure would crumble down on them. They set up a wild clamor of shrieks and yells, audible to the crowds outside. An assessment of the damage revealed that although a quantity of brick was torn out by the explosion, a complete hole through the jail wall was not made, and no prisoners escaped.

Fernekes denied placing the bomb, denied that he had made a beeline for the spot immediately after the explosion and asserted that he had stood calmly by until order was restored. On searching his cell, guards found a cup of paraffin that had recently been heated by matches and a handful of nitro powder. Fernekes was charged.

On August 16, seven prisoners attempted to break out. They had sawed through the bars and were pushing themselves through when a guard called for help. A riot squad rushed to his assistance. Fernekes was thought to be the instigator. The jail was in turmoil in the aftermath. Guards were discharged and suspended. A court investigation of jail conditions was started, and Warden George P. Weideling resigned. Fernekes was said to be the most desperate criminal in the jail. He had been in solitary confinement for some time but somehow managed to have smuggled in material that might be used to escape.

In December 1926, the judge who had sentenced Fernekes to death, before the decision was reversed by the Supreme Court, received a Christmas greeting from Henry Ferneckes: "Cordial greetings and all good wishes for Christmas." Later, when the assistant state's attorney who had obtained Ferneke's conviction was murdered, the Midget wrote to former state attorney Robert E. Crowe: "Although I have nothing in common with the state's attorney's office, yet I feel called upon to condole you in the loss of a brilliant and conscientious member of your staff."

Fernekes was taken from the Cook County jail to Joliet Penitentiary. On May 1, 1927, police uncovered a plan to kidnap the grandchild of the late Chicago millionaire John G. Shedd of Marshall Field & Co. John Shedd Schweippe, nine, or his sister, Jean, eleven, were apparently going to be held for ransom. The plan was to raise funds for the defense of Henry J. "Midget" Fernekes. Mrs. Jessie Mulhall Saunders, who had been known as Mrs.

Darche at the time of the Pearl River robbery, was identified by Charles H. Schweppe, father of the intended victims, as a woman he had seen prowling about the grounds of his Lake Forest estate.

"Seven well known gunmen were involved" police said. They were all members of the band that kidnapped two cabaret owners and finally released them for a reported ransom of $100,000. Private detectives—twenty-four armed men in three eight-hour shifts—maintained their heavy guard over the palatial Schweppe estate. Equipped with automobiles and private telephones, they were questioning everyone who came near the mansion.

In July, news articles across the country ran headlines including "Midget—The Ultra Modern Bandit and Crook" and "Death Beckons One of the Brainiest Men in Country—Because He's a Crook." The articles summarized Fernekes's career with sensational spin. "New Type Super Desperado is a Dapper Person—He makes the arts and science an adjunct to meteoric life of crime." The glamorization continued, "He is one of the most amazing criminals of this age. He studied in art schools and libraries, seeking knowledge that might enable him better to pursue success in his chosen nefarious profession."

On August 1, 1927, New York asked for extradition again. The district attorney from Rockland County, New York, had said before that if Fernekes got anything but the death penalty, they would seek extradition. The charge of murder in Illinois had been dropped for lack of evidence, and Fernekes was now serving from ten years to life for robbery. New York had him on two murders and wanted justice and extradition papers.

In April 1929, a west side dentist was executed in his office. Investigators uncovered a connection between Dr. Brady and the Fernekes's robbery gang. A search of the dentist's office revealed acids and other materials used by criminals to alter the engraving on bonds and securities. They also found evidence of unlawful traffic in narcotics.

Mid-afternoon on August 3, 1935, a man entered the interview room where visitors were received at Joliet Prison. The man, wearing a white shirt, tweed cap and smoked glasses, presented a card with the name and number of his prisoner friend, George Ammen. A clerk directed the visitor to seek the man at the new prison—a separate structure across the city. Still bearing the card, the man left. When he reached the prison wall, the guard touched his cap politely as he unbarred the gates and allowed the man to leave. Henry J. Fernekes walked through the gates and disappeared. When the escape was made known, armed guards began a hunt of the surrounding country, and a warning was sent to police headquarters in Chicago to be on

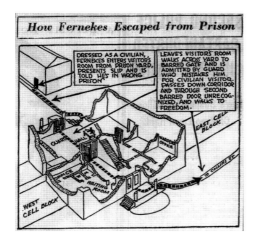

"How Fernekes Escaped from Prison."
Chicago Tribune, *August 4, 1935.*

the lookout for the fugitive. Four prison guards who knew Fernekes by sight were dispatched to places where it was thought that he might go. They were sure, however, that Fernekes had probably made detailed arrangements for his getaway before he walked out of the prison gate.

The guards were questioned under the lie detector. Fernekes slipped out of the shop some time before 1:30 p.m. on Saturday, but a guard admitted he did not miss the convict until nearly 4:00 p.m. He informed Assistant Warden George F. Schring, who ordered a search of the entire prison.

After slipping out of his work duty, Fernekes put on a blue denim suit that he had bleached and hidden near the powerhouse in preparation for his escape. Convicts had reported seeing a civilian strolling about the prison yard with a roll of paper that appeared to be an architect's blueprints and examining the buildings. Presuming that this man was engaged in construction work, neither convicts nor guards took further notice of him. Fernekes then slipped into the visitors' room.

Four guards were suspended for "inefficiency and negligence in discharge of their duty," declared Bowen. "We are convinced there was no bribery or collusion, only gross stupidity." Governor Horner ordered by telegraph that a $1,000 reward be offered for Fernekes's capture—the maximum authorized by law.

On duty in the visitors' room was Michael Leonard, captain of the guards, who was relieving Captain Charles Rogers for a short time. Guards on duty at the two gates in the administration building indicated that Leonard had pressed the buzzer that rang at their posts and indicated to them that the departing visitor was all right. The guard who let him out said later, "I didn't remember letting that man in, but I supposed he must have come in while

I was at lunch. I noticed that he had some sort of white substance on his upper lip." Sehring recalled that Fernekes had a sore spot on his upper lip and had been treated with a white caustic. Though there were discrepancies in the guards' testimonies—details and times that did not exactly match up—Governor Horner and Warden Whipp declared that the lie detector charts had shown no deviations from normal.

Two weeks after the escape, it was decided that the visiting room would be removed from the penitentiary yard to a guard hall and another barred gate added to the route that visitors must follow when leaving the prison. Any person desiring to leave money for a convict must properly identify himself. That such a rule was not in effect at Joliet or the other state prisons came to light when authorities realized that Fernekes had been playing the stock market during his last two years in prison. The money was left in the warden's office by "a friend," according to the prison records. At one time, this unnamed donor left him $72.50 and at another $500. This money was used to conduct an account with two Chicago brokerage concerns. According to these companies, his profit was over $1,000. This money was sent out of the prison by Fernekes to some other "friends." No effort was made to trace it or learn if the valuables were turned over to underworld connections to pave the way for Ferneckes's escape.

On August 7, Warden Frank D. Whipp received a letter signed with the name Midget Fernekes under the space for the return address. The letter bore a Joliet postmark and was mailed the day before. It said:

> *Dear Warden,*
> *You were all good to me. Too many men my reason for giving more room.*
> *However, I still like Joliet and am hereabouts.*
> *Midget*

More than twenty thousand circulars were sent to banks warning them to be on their guard. Whipp resigned; though he gave other reasons, it was assumed that the embarrassing escape was to blame.

When Fernekes was finally recaptured, he told the chief of detectives, "Hell, I'd rather go back to New York and face the chair than to Joliet." The next morning, he was unconscious on the floor of his cell. He died before reaching the hospital. He'd taken a lethal dose of poison to avoid returning to prison.

In 1936, CBS ran a radio program called "Gang Busters," featuring the case of Henry "Midget" Fernekes.

VACEK'S PARDON

Chief Justice McKinley of the criminal court wrote to the governor to ask for help for Joseph Vacek—a man the judge had sentenced seven years before (in 1914) to twenty-five years in prison: "The interests of the public will not suffer if you use executive clemency in this case." Vacek had killed his father because, he claimed, his father had urged him to kill his own mother so that the senior Vacek could have more time for an affinity.

The sixteen-year-old later escaped from Joliet. He went to Chicago and married a maid he met while working in a hospital. He was arrested after three years of freedom and returned to a cell. McKinley and others assured Governor Small that the slaying of his father was in defense of Vacek's mother and that he had "gone straight."

Mrs. Lena Vacek told reporters, "I am happier than I can say at the way in which so many prominent men and women have come to the aid of myself, my husband and our little son in our trouble. I, too, am told that the chances are very good that the governor will pardon Joe immediately and send him back to me." She won her husband back from the state's prison at Joliet in September 1922.

LEOPOLD AND LOEB

Nathan Leopold Jr. and Richard Albert Loeb were two nineteen-year-old students from wealthy families who were studying at the University of Chicago. On May 21, 1924, they kidnapped and murdered fourteen-year-old Bobby Franks. They believed themselves capable of carrying out the "perfect crime" because of their intellectual superiority.

Bobby Franks was the son of wealthy Chicago watch manufacturer Jacob Franks. He was also Richard Loeb's second cousin and across-the-street neighbor. The two men lured Bobby into a car as he was leaving the Harvard School for Boys at about 5:00 p.m. They drove him to a suburban forest preserve and pounded a chisel into his head. Bobby's mother told police that she received a call that night from a man who said the boy had been kidnapped and was safe. The next morning, Bobby's father received a mailed note instructing him to send $10,000 ransom. Later that morning, the child's nude body was found stuffed into a railroad culvert. Not far away, a pair of shell-rimmed glasses that were later identified as belonging to Leopold were recovered.

Richard Loeb, eighteen (*left*), and Nathan Leopold Jr., nineteen, look at each other after they gave separate confessions to the May 21, 1924 killing of Bobby Franks in Chicago. Chicago Tribune *historical photo*.

At first, Leopold and Loeb gloried in the notoriety. When pinned down, each accused the other of the murder. Leopold whined that lethal weapons were so abhorrent to him that handling them brought on nausea, but it was known that he shot birds for sport. Leopold thought to bribe a juror, and Loeb thought his father's money would get him off with two or three years in jail. He told reporters that he would emerge a "new man."

The trial for what was called the "crime of the century" was a media frenzy. Loeb's family retained Clarence Darrow as lead counsel for the defense. Concluding that a jury trial would end in conviction and the death penalty, Darrow advised them to enter guilty pleas, hoping for sentences of life imprisonment. The sentencing hearing took thirty-two days. Both Leopold and Loeb were sentenced to life imprisonment, plus ninety-nine years.

Leopold and Loeb began serving their sentences at Joliet Prison on September 11, 1924. They spent their first night in the court solitary, where all prisoners began their stay in the penitentiary. On Monday, Richard Loeb started to work in the prison chair factory, Nathan Leopold in the rattan factory. They were kept apart as much as possible but managed to maintain their friendship behind bars. Leopold was transferred to Stateville in 1927. Loeb followed in 1931.

On January 28, 1936, Loeb was attacked by another convict, James Day, with a straight razor in a shower room. His throat was slashed from behind. He had more than fifty wounds, including defensive wounds on his arms and hands. He died soon after in the prison hospital. News accounts implied that Loeb had propositioned Day, though it was more likely that Day had attacked Loeb after his advances were rebuffed. Prison authorities ruled that Day had been defending himself. Day was later tried and acquitted of Loeb's murder.

On February 5, 1958, Leopold addressed the Illinois Parole and Pardon Board, saying, "I am an old man, a broken man, who pleads for your compassion. I want a chance to find redemption for myself and to help others. I know I can do more good outside." He had participated in the 1944 malaria study at Stateville, which was to benefit him when parole was considered.

According to Illinois law, Leopold would have to have "honorable and useful employment" and a "proper and suitable home free from criminal influence and without expense to the state." He wanted to work for a mountain

Clarence Darrow in 1924 with his clients, Nathan Leopold (*left*) and Richard Loeb. *United Press International.*

hospital in Puerto Rico that had offered him ten dollars a month and living expenses. A meeting was held, and a motion in favor of the Leopold parole was made. He was granted parole on February 20. The board also voted unanimously to grant Roger Touhy, Prohibition-era gangster, parole on one of two sentences he was serving. The two men's stories were run side by side in newspapers across the country.

Leopold served thirty-three years in prison. After many unsuccessful parole petitions, he was released in March 1958. He was accepted as a medical technician at a hospital in Puerto Rico by the Brethren Service Commission. Known as "Nate," he worked at Castaner General Hospital as a laboratory and X-ray assistant. Leopold later said, "The Brethren Service Commission offered the job, the home, and the sponsorship without which a man cannot be paroled. But it gave me so much more than that, the companionship, the acceptance, the love which would have rendered a violation of parole almost impossible." Leopold later married a widowed florist.

He earned a master's degree at the University of Puerto Rico and later taught classes there. He did research in the social service program of Puerto Rico's department of health and worked for an urban renewal and housing agency. He performed research on leprosy at the University of Puerto Rico's school of medicine. In 1963, Nathan Leopold returned to Chicago to attend meetings of the American Society of Parasitologists and the American Society of Tropical Hygiene and Medicine.

Leopold died at Mimya Hospital in Santurce, Puerto Rico, on August 28, 1971, at the age of sixty-six. According to his wife, Trudi, he had been suffering from congestive heart failure.

STATEVILLE

When Stateville was completed in 1925, it was thought that it was only a matter of time until the Old Prison in Joliet was closed. But the Prohibition amendment brought a rising crime rate during the 1920s and '30s that demanded more prisons, and Joliet was saved.

ELSIE SWEETIN

Elsie was taken to the women's prison at Joliet on January 6, 1925. Her last statement, made the night before, was to deny the published report that she had admitted having become engaged to the minister Reverend Lawrence Hight, who poisoned his wife and Elsie's husband to win her love. She said that he had purchased an engagement ring for her even before her husband had died. Hight was taken to the Southern Illinois Penitentiary at Chester to begin his life sentence. Sweetin, who was charged with complicity in the poisoning of her husband, was sentenced to thirty-five years in prison.

JAMES SAMMONS

James "Fur" Sammons was one of the key figures of the old Capone gang. He was convicted in 1903 (when he was just nineteen) of the murder of a saloonkeeper and sentenced to death. The death sentence was commuted, and Sammons went to prison to serve a life term. In 1922, Governor Len Small commuted the sentence to fifty years, which made Sammons eligible for parole, having served one-third of the fifty years. He was said by his associates to have become "stir crazy." They asserted that he "loved to hear the noise of a machine gun."

In 1925, he walked into a northwest side saloon that was taking bootleg beer from a gang in competition with the Capones. Witnesses said Sammons turned his machine gun loose and riddled a dozen beer barrels. He worked for the Capone gang, the Touhy gang and other beer racketeers in the ten years of Prohibition, until 1933. He was in trouble frequently, and his parole was finally revoked. He was taken back to prison but obtained his release on a court order.

In 1926, he was questioned by the Cook County grand jury investigating the murder of William McSwiggin, assistant state's attorney, and two companions. Sammons was held on a charge of participating in an $80,000 International Harvester company payroll robbery. He was also reported to have been in McSwiggin's car when it was riddled with machine gun bullets. He was taken before the grand jury against his will and at the time that he surrendered to police was suffering from five bullet wounds. He refused to sign an immunity waiver and was closeted with the jurors for about forty minutes. John Capone, a brother of "Scarface" Al Capone, was arrested as a result of the McSwiggin investigation, and authorities searched in vain for Scarface.

Sammons was convicted in 1934 of attempting to bribe a policeman in Indiana. He was imprisoned there for several years and then was turned back to Illinois and imprisoned in Joliet Penitentiary. He was ordered paroled again in 1952 and went to live with his brother in Chicago. He was nearly blind when released and had been bedfast for his last several years in prison because of a heart condition. On May 19, 1960, he checked in to the Englewood Arms hotel. The next morning, when the maid entered to make the bed, she found the seventy-six-year-old man dead. He was not known to the hotel personnel as the Prohibition-era gangster.

GRANDMA NUSSBAUM

For the love of an ex-convict with whom she had been carrying on an affair for fifteen years, Eliza Nussbaum, fifty-nine, grandmother of eight children, plotted the murder of her husband. Albert, sixty-five, a well-to-do contractor, was slain on December 29, 1925, in the home of Delilah Martin, who catered to roomers.

Eliza admitted the crime to police following her arrest. After telling of her love affair with John Winn, she said, "Albert wasn't dying fast enough." She named three accomplices and outlined the plan. She said that she had tried to back out at the last minute, but they wouldn't let her. She said, "When I came home last night, my husband was not there, and I knew that they had done it." She said that she and Winn had planned to marry after she had obtained her husband's money. Nussbaum was considered wealthy, owning half a dozen apartment buildings, as well as a prosperous contracting business.

Early the next day, police saw a fire at Ninety-Fourth Street and Branton Avenue on the far South Side. Investigation disclosed a body in a snowdrift in a mass of flaming paper and rags. An undertaker identified the body, and police took Nussbaum's twenty-year-old grandson, Lloyd, into custody. A piece of the victim's skull and bloodstains were found in a car that Lloyd was driving. Lloyd's father, Roscoe, unwilling to see his son subjected to a torturous examination by police, betrayed his own mother with the assertion that she was in love with an ex-convict.

Edward Goff, friend of the Nussbaum family, confessed to the actual slaying. He and his cousin Marion Stringham had kidnapped Nussbaum. While Stringham covered the old man with his revolver, Goff declared that he himself struck him over the head with a club. The two carried the body to the Nussbaum garage and when darkness fell conveyed it to the prairie, where it was found at dawn the next day.

Police arrested Nussbaum and then Goff, Mrs. Martin and Marion Springham, a roomer at the Martin home. Nussbaum told police that her husband's cruelty drove her to plot his death. The woman said that she became acquainted with Winn some sixteen years before, when her husband had an affair with the ex-convict's wife.

Nussbaum said that in the forty-four years of their married life, her sixty-five-year-old paralytic husband's one kind act was to buy her ice cream once, while John Winn loved her and waited fifteen years for him to die. A diary was found in her purse in which she expressed fear that her husband would kill her.

John Walton Winn, forty-seven, who had served a penitentiary sentence in 1914 for robbery, was arrested at Crown Point, Indiana, the next day and brought to Chicago for examination. When Winn was arrested, police found a letter from Nussbaum giving instructions for the murder. Winn denied the affair, saying that she had only been like a mother to him and treated him as her son. Prospective jurors were asked if they could return a hanging verdict against Grandma if they believed she was guilty, even if she was a woman.

On January 4, after four days of denials that earned him the name "Granite Man," John Winn added his confession to those of the other four. He charged that Goff, not he, wielded the hammer with which Nussbaum was beaten to death. Winn's breakdown came after Mrs. Nussbaum had kissed him and begged him to tell everything. "I might as well," he said. "I guess I'm going to hang anyway."

On March 6, a jury deliberated for three hours and twenty minutes before reaching a verdict. "Grandma" Nussbaum was found guilty and sentenced to life in prison. John Winn was sentenced to hang. When the decision was read, the newspaper reported that "Winn's smile turned to a frown and Nussbaum fainted."

Poultry Theft

On July 22, 1926, pretty Louise Porter, a seventeen-year-old high school girl from Villa Grove, Illinois, entered to serve one to twenty years in the women's prison. It seemed that a honeymoon elopement had ended at the doors of the women's prison. Three weeks before, Louise, a junior at Villa Grove High School, ran away from home to marry Frank Porter. He had been cruising around Villa Grove in a high-powered car. Porter, his bride and another man were arrested on a charge of stealing chickens after three crates of chickens were found in Porter's car. He was arrested at Casey, Illinois, and tried before a jury at Marshall in Clark County.

In Clark County and the southern section of the state, chicken stealing was looked on as a serious crime due to the numerous inroads made on poultry houses in that section. Mrs. Porter and her husband were found guilty of burglary and larceny and sentenced to one to twenty years in the penitentiary. The young girl's husband was sent to Chester while she was brought to the women's prison.

HAROLD CROARKIN

Twenty-six-year-old Harold Croarkin was the son of a wealthy flour manufacturer, but he was known to people in his neighborhood as a "goof." He had a twin that was "normal," but Harold had played with a ragdoll until he was fourteen years old. On December 17, 1926, Harold went to two Catholic priests and told them that he thought he had killed a boy. He led them to the Devon Riding Club, where they found the child in a hayloft, clinging to life. While the priests were administering first aid to the little boy and preparing to rush him to a hospital, Croarkin fled. The child died several hours after being taken to St. Francis Hospital in Evanston.

Croarkin walked into the police station a week later and surrendered. He was accompanied by his uncle, Francis E. Croarkin, who was a former school trustee. Croarkin confessed that he beat the child on the head with a hammer but denied molesting him. "I killed him—I don't know why I did it." Croarkin, a slim youth of less than average height and wearing heavy shell-rimmed glasses, denied that he was mentally challenged or abnormal in any way. Questioned further, the youth said, "I was just mad at him. I hit him twice over the head with something." Fearing violence against the prisoner, police loaded Croarkin into an automobile and hustled him over to the Summerdale station, where the jail was more secure.

Croarkin was arrested three months before on the complaint of the father of an eight-year-old girl. The youth denied any improper motives and declared he intended the girl no harm. Harold was frightened by the police and promised fervently that such a thing would never, never happen again. He was told that if he was ever arrested for the same offense, he would be sent to the penitentiary. But he had returned to his perversities. After his arrest for murder, he admitted twelve offenses in three months—half of them boys and half girls. These had not come to the attention of the police because the families involved did not care to have the matter become public, or because they themselves had not known what happened.

Playmates of
Walter Schmith act
as pallbearers at his
funeral. Chicago
Daily Tribune,
December 21, 1926.

The odd man was said to be a puzzling combination of remorse and indifference. At times, he was on the verge of collapse, then quickly rallying, would comment casually about the weather and other commonplace subjects. Once or twice he even laughed. He was questioned at length by State Attorney Crowe in the presence of Drs. William O. Krok and N. Douglas Singer, alienists, both of whom were witnesses at the trial of Leopold and Loeb. Attorneys for the slayer entered a defense of insanity at the trial, but a half-dozen psychiatrists testified that Croarkin was sane. He had good marks in school and had shown business aptitude as a salesman for his father.

At the trial, he seemed unmoved by the witnesses. He sat slouched in a chair with one foot resting on the round of a chair in front of him, gazing idly around the courtroom. Mrs. Walter Schmith identified the cap her son had worn the day he was murdered, but Croarkin gave no hint of emotion. The defendant did not take the witness stand. As expected, the defense presented a battery of experts to prove that the prisoner was mentally defective. X-ray pictures of Croarkin's body were placed on view, and Dr. Maxmilian J. Hubeny testified that the defendant was so small as nearly to equal the minimum for a human. He said the thymus should have appeared as only a remnant in one of Croarkin's age but was of tumbrous growth and had pushed aside the windpipe and the aorta, the main trunk of the arterial system. Harold had a stunted pituitary gland, a persistent thymus and only four of the customary five-lumbar vertebrae.

Dr. William J. Hickson, head of the Cook County Psychopathic Hospital, testified that Croarkin suffered from dementia praecox with tendencies toward mania and dementia. He stated that it was his opinion that the young man had been insane when he killed Walter Schmith. "I applied psychological and neurological tests to the prisoner," he said. "Though I find his intelligence average, I found him very suggestible, as in all cases of his type, and very, very weak willed. I found no adequate emotional reaction, and disharmonies between his intelligence and his emotions. His laughs are silly and unmotivated, typical of dementia praecox."

The most sensational expert testimony was given by the Reverend Dr. Thomas Moore, head of the department of psychology at the Catholic University at Washington, D.C., and consulting psychiatrist at the Mount Hope Asylum for the Insane at Baltimore. Dr. Moore stated that it was quite likely that Harold's mental and physical deficiencies were the result of lack of proper nourishment before his birth. He pointed out that Harold's twin sister, Hortense, was an unusually robust young woman and that very probably she had received an oversupply of prenatal nourishment while her brother had received an undersupply. "My opinion," said Dr. Moore, "based upon my examination, upon his personal history, his absolute indifference to the enormity of the act he committed, his complete lack of remorse or regret, is that Harold Croarkin was insane at the time of the murder and is now insane."

State Attorney Robert E. Crowe, who had provided the fireworks in the Leopold and Loeb case, attacked the findings of the defense alienists. In his summation, he said, "One defense alienist says Croarkin was a victim of dementia praecox since his birth twenty-six years ago. Another defense alienist says his mental deterioration set in just last fall. One defense attorney tells you that this case is so involved that no twelve jurors can fathom its intricacies and it should be decided by expert psychiatrists. Another defense attorney would convince you that it is so simple a case that no doctor is needed, that any twelve men could tell that Croarkin is insane. These are futile attempts to confuse you and aid this man to escape the gallows."

Crowe continually dwelt on the idea that this defendant had known right from wrong when he committed his crime and therefore was sane in the eyes of the law. He pleaded with the jury to return a verdict of murder in the first degree and a sentence of death. He said that only thus would little boys and little girls be properly protected from fiends who prowl at large, seeking victims for their depravities. In conclusion, he said, "If this is not a hanging case, you might as well abolish the penalty. In the murder of a six-year-old boy by a depraved man, there can be no extenuating circumstances." The jury deliberated two hours and then returned a compromise verdict that found Harold Croarkin guilty and sent him to Joliet Penitentiary for life. Harold J. Croarkin died on November 20, 1954, at Stateville Penitentiary.

BROADWAY

Kitty Malm was accused of participating in the murder of a night watchman during a holdup committed by her common-law husband, Otto Malm, and another man. Lonely for her daughter, "Tootsie," Kitty surrendered to authorities in 1923. During Kitty's sensational trial, she was nicknamed the "Tiger Girl." Newspapers revealed that she'd come from Austria when she was seven years old. She was married at fifteen to Max Baluk, the father of her daughter. Kitty was sentenced to life imprisonment. She entered the prison on May 29, 1924. She never went beyond the fifth grade in school but in prison studied typewriting and shorthand and worked as a clerk in the prison office.

At the time of Kitty's trial, she was housed on "Murderesses' Row" in the Cook County Jail with several other female murderers. *Chicago Tribune*

Katherine "Kitty" Malm and daughter Tootsie, February 20, 1924. *Chicago History Press.*

reporter Maurine Watkins covered the trials of these women and later made millions on a play she wrote based on their stories. The play later became the Broadway sensation *Chicago*, with song lyrics like "he had it comin'."

Beulah Annan (the inspiration for Roxie Hart) was a beautiful twenty-three-year-old who claimed self-defense after she shot "the other man to the tune of her husband's phonograph." Watkins wrote that Beulah, "whose pursuit of wine, men, and jazz music was interrupted by her glibness with the trigger finger, was given freedom…by her 'beauty-proof' jury."

Belva Gaertner (the inspiration for Velma Kelly) shot a man to death "with a steel bullet after a cabaret gin party." She claimed she was too drunk to remember what had happened when she was found covered in blood near the murder scene. She was touted in the press as "Cook County's most stylish defendant," with descriptions of her elaborate wardrobe.

The innocent Hungarian ballerina in the show was inspired by Sabella Nitti, a recent Italian immigrant who was arrested for the murder of her missing husband. She was found guilty and was the first woman sentenced to hang in Chicago but was later cleared of the murder. She and "Go-to-Hell-Kitty" were especially close and supported each other while they could. On December 27, 1932, Kitty died of pneumonia in the women's prison at Joliet. She was only twenty-eight years old.

MOONSHINE MARY IN PEN FOR SELLING HOOTCH

In February 1927, thirty-four-year-old "Moonshine Mary" Wazenlak was taken to the women's prison at Joliet to begin serving a sentence from one year to life in connection with the death of one of four men who died from the effects of liquor made and sold by her. The mother of three children was said to be the first woman in Illinois to be convicted of a charge of selling fatal moonshine.

BANDETTES—GANGS OF GIRLS ROAM CHICAGO

In May 1927, newspapers announced that "gunning for money" had become a feminine game in Lake City. The increasing number of flapper bandits alarmed civic workers. "It is thought probable that the 'bandettes' are recruited from the rings of gangland (Early)." They speculated that there were twenty-one gangs composed entirely of girls roaming Chicago.

"Moonshine Mary" Wazenlak was arrested for selling moonshine to a man who later died, circa March 1924. *Chicago History Press.*

J.H. English, supervisor of recreation for the board of education, made this "fact" public in connection with an investigation into child life conditions. He discovered 226 playground gangs. Of these, 205 were composed of boys; the rest were girls. Social service workers saw a direct connection between this condition and the increasing number of women figuring in crimes of violence. Some names mentioned in the articles were Pearl Dorsey, twenty, who carried a gun and was arrested on charges of holding up a taxi. Violet Hammond was sentenced to one to ten years for participating in stickups. Jean Hunter was sentenced to three to twenty years for banditry.

FLORENCE SCHROEDER

While Florence Schroeder's husband stayed at home and minded their ten-month-old son, Florence, seventeen, was arrested when the two men that were with her attempted to hold up a taxicab driver. One of the men saw a detective bureau squad car approaching and fled. Harry Mendel, twenty-two, was arrested with Schroeder. She said she met him the afternoon before. She denied that she knew her companion intended to rob. Mendel's pistol was found in the taxicab.

FRANCES VAUGHN

Frances Vaughn was arrested on charges of participating in a holdup. The sullen, sorrowful girl gave police what was obviously an alias, saying it would serve as well as any other name. Ernest de Lavergne had been wounded in the frustrated robbery of a car barn. The twenty-one-year-old would be crippled for life if he lived to go to the penitentiary. Ernest's brother Joseph and an ex-convict named William Mullowney were killed in that holdup project.

Frances was the only one to face police questioning. She alone was a prisoner, alive and unwounded. The other girl of the robber's party, known as Marie Nolan, had escaped. Ernest de Lavergne had escaped the car station where Lieutenant John Norton and a squad had awaited the coming of the robbers, having been informed that the robbery was planned. But when police caught Ernest a few hours later, Frances bartered her silence for the opportunity of seeing him and talking with him. Ernest De Lavergne was brought to Acting Chief John Stege's office on a litter, and Frances ran sobbing to his side, covering his face with kisses, as he assured her that he would not die.

Ernest had admitted his part in the robbery that failed—the robbers never reaching the $19,000 turned in to the office by conductors—how it was planned, who planned it and the part each took. "I'll take whatever he gets; I'll ask no favors," the girl informed Chief Stege. She continued:

> I could have escaped when Marie did, but I wouldn't go till I learned what had happened to Ernie. That's the only reason I went along last night; I'd rather be there to see for myself than to be home worrying about what might happen to him. Ernie was good to me. I was working in a restaurant. I needed financial help so I accepted his offer to live in his apartment.

> *The one that proposed the robbery to Ernest backed out at the last minute and informed the police.* [Chief Stege said this was not correct.] *But Ernie wouldn't back out. His brother came Sunday evening with this Mullowney and the girl—I heard her name was Marie Nolan—and she was driving the car. I think it was hers.*
>
> *Then we went to the car station on Noble Street and the boys went in. Marie and I stayed in the car. When the shooting started, a policeman* [Sergeant James Hacksa] *grabbed me. He pulled me from the car and Marie drove away.*

She confessed but wouldn't give her name, saying that she didn't want her folks to hear of her arrest. The police, however, guessed at a possible identification. In September 1922, a fifteen-year-old girl had been arrested as a drug user. She was Frances Quinn of Bucklin, Missouri, a town with a population of 2,500. She was visiting relatives in Oak Park and had been arrested on their complaint when she stayed out several nights. This girl was taken to the juvenile home. A picture of Frances Quinn bore a striking resemblance to Frances Vaughn.

HELEN KONKEL

On July 5, 1927, Helen Konkel, "Bandit Queen," was sentenced to three to twenty years in prison when she and three male associates pled guilty to charges of robbery. Carl Swenson, because of his age, was sentenced to one to ten years, while the other two received sentences similar to Helen's. She was called "Hardboiled" Helen by the police. But on July 8, her sentence was cut in half by Judge John J. Sullivan in the criminal court. Several days before, the judge refused to listen to her plea for leniency, telling her that she was lucky she was not fighting to escape the gallows instead of the penitentiary. At that time, he imposed a sentence from three to twenty years. The charge was changed to robbery and the sentence to one to ten years. The "Gun Girl" was arrested after a $7,000 jewelry store holdup.

Certainly, early associations played a part in the forming of those women's characters. The gang organization was seen as a steppingstone to crime. "These gangs," English said, "are composed largely of two groups of young people. The first group is made up of members of about fourteen years of age, the adolescent age. The ages of the second group average seventeen, the post-adolescent age." The fourteen-year-olds were mischievous. The

JOLIET PRISON BLUES

older ones were not infrequently vicious. Many of the groups were brought under the direction of playground directors. But fully half were running wild, operating classes for crime, in the opinions of investigators.

EDA PETERSON BOGIE

In January 1928, Eda Peterson Bogie was wanted in Davenport, Iowa, on a first-degree murder charge stemming from the mysterious death of her adopted son, Harold Barker Bogie, in January 1926. About that same time, Eda had been arrested for obtaining goods by false pretenses. She had been charging merchandise in Moline and Rock Island stores to a woman for whom she once did domestic work. On her release following this sentence, authorities promised to be on hand to take her into custody for questioning about her son's death.

NEW INVENTIONS ARE BREEDERS OF CRIME

On November 12, 1926, an article ran in the newspapers reporting that the commissioner of correction for Massachusetts and president of the American Prison Association, Sanford Bates, said that the general volume of crime was on the downward trend in the United States. This seemed laughable to the newspapermen, who responded:

> *Mr. Bates should be in a position to know...but when a man makes such a statement as this, we can hardly keep from asking ourselves what sort of an out-of-the-way occurrence Mr. Bates records as a crime? If embezzlement, mail robberies and bootlegging are to be placed in this category it would seem that crime is on anything but a decline. Mr. Bates says that vagrancy and drunkenness have decreased in the last ten years—that these historic breeders of crime are on the downward path once and for all. He must believe that idle hands and illicit liquor have ceased to cause the lawlessness that we hear about. Certainly, this is not the case. It never has been and it seems highly probable that it ever will be. "New inventions are breeders of crime, but then we do not know what grandfather would have done with the latest inventions," says Mr. Bates. However, it is not a long flight for the imagination to picture grandfather doing much the same as is being done today. Mr. Bates says that there are no criminals of the Jesse James type*

in the United States today, but it does not take a Jesse James to commit a crime. The characters of today are different and their methods dissimilar to those employed by the old notorious criminals, but the results are much the same.

Martin Durkin, who made front page copy by his threats to shoot it out with the police, and who became somewhat of a temporary hero because of his florid affairs with women, went into Joliet prison where he is to spend the next half century for the murder of a federal agent. He was no longer the bizarre "sheik," but just another criminal whom the law had caught. When first captured in St. Louis, he gaily posed for newspaper pictures. Saturday, he dropped his head with "you'se guys have got enough of me." They had—the curtain had been rung down on his act. He was considered typical of the criminal produced by new inventions, but his history does not vary to any great extent from that of the "bad man" of years ago. Mr. Bates may be right, we hope he is. But if the volume has become smaller, hasn't the quality become more serious?

Oldest Prisoner Turns Ninety-Eight

"Old Charlie" Lindwall, the oldest prisoner in Joliet Penitentiary and possibly the oldest in the country observed his ninety-eighth birthday on May 11, 1927. He was sentenced to life in prison in 1900 for murder, which he denied committing. The court told him his age alone had saved him from the gallows. Since then, the judge and most of the jurors had died, but Charlie lived on. "Half blind, feeble, and bowed with his years, [he] has clung to life, serving his penalty with borrowed time over the allotted three score years and ten." It was said that he puttered around the prison yard each day, the guards and prisoners mostly leaving him alone. He enjoyed a movie on Saturday morning and chapel on Sunday. He refused a pardon a few years before, maintaining that he was too old to face the world.

An Unpriestly Imposter

On May 11, 1927, William Evans was arrested when he tried to drive an automobile in the gates of the prison while posing as a missionary priest. When he asked admittance to give aid to some of the inmates, the guard at the gate became suspicious and called the deputy warden. Four other men who followed the automobile in another car sped away. The "priest" tried to escape, but guards overpowered him and retrieved a revolver from his pocket. As guards began to search the car, they soon uncovered nitroglycerine, mustard gas bombs, firearms, three complete outfits of clothing and a blueprint.

The man would not tell officials who he was attempting to liberate, so additional guards were placed near the cells of Richard Loeb, Henry Fernekes, Warren Lincoln and Harold Croarkin—inmates thought to be the target of Evans's plan. Detectives came from Chicago to try to identify him. A lodge card bore the name Harry L. Sullivan of Cripple Creek, Colorado, and the automobile had a Michigan license. In one of the suits of clothing was found a slip of paper bearing the name Henry Funk.

Funk had been sentenced to life in prison for robbing a Chenoa, Illinois bank of $108,000. He and a partner had posed as bank examiners, spending most of the day in the bank. After closing hours, the robbers had bound and gagged bank officials and escaped with cash and negotiable securities. Funk was later arrested in Champaign, Illinois.

According to the bureau of identification records, Evans was convict no. 22021 at Jefferson City, serving a life sentence for a murder in Kansas City in 1919. He had escaped from the Missouri prison on August 9, 1923, while working as an assistant in the prison hospital. Henry Funk had helped William Evans escape—Evans hoped to now "repay the favor." Ironically, Funk was not confined at the old prison where Evans had tried to break in. He had been removed to the new prison at Stateville, several miles away. The next day, William "Mike" Evans was returned to the state penitentiary at Jefferson City, Missouri.

NEW INSTRUMENT OF DEATH

In December 1928, the electric chair was used for the first time in Illinois. Dominic Bressetti, a Chippewa Indian; John Brown; and Claude Clark were electrocuted shortly after 7:00 a.m. for the murder of Will Beck, a Lake County farmer. Clark was led to the chair at 7:12 a.m. and pronounced dead six minutes later. Brown followed, and Bressetti was the last to die. Twelve men from Waukegan, the scene of the trial, witnessed the execution. Warden Elmer J. Green and four deputy wardens were in the death chamber.

Beck was slain in the door of his home when the trio attempted to rob him. Brown shot him. Bressetti began the conspiracy to rob Beck when he came to Chicago with money lent to him by Beck, his prospective employer. He told Brown and Clark of Beck's hidden money. Two men hired to drive the trio to Beck's home were convicted of manslaughter. Bressetti, a World War I veteran, surrendered and confessed to Chicago police.

GALESBURG MAN NAMED WARDEN

Major Henry C. Hill succeeded Elmer J. Green as the warden of the Joliet and Stateville Penitentiaries. He was a veteran of the Spanish-American War and was a major of infantry in World War I. He was a Secret Service operative and post office inspector before the war. He was also a "city inspector" in New York City from 1900 to 1909. Since 1915, he had been in business in Galesburg, following foreign service for a New York business house.

In a statement of policy, Major Hill said he had accepted the post at the request of Governor Emmerson "because we are in harmony in realizing that there may be vast improvement eventually made in the prisons of the country. Neither of us has any pet theories to experiment with," he said. "We believe that the state in the broad sense of theory should use its power mercifully—by human endeavors to reform and improve those upon whom it has laid its hands. We fear no outbreaks such as have taken place in some of the penal institutions throughout the country, because the occupants of the Illinois prisons are well treated and adequately housed and provided for. During the past few weeks, many measures have been taken by state authorities to enable prison officers to quell instantly any attempt on the part of the prisoners either to riot or escape." There were approximately 3,700 convicts in the state prison and at Stateville as the new warden took over his office. A new cell house was soon to be built to relieve crowded conditions.

Hill arrived on August 12, 1929, with Colonel Frank D. Whipp, assistant director of the state department of public welfare. They went immediately to the state prison, where an inspection was made. He quickly realized that the facilities were grossly overcrowded and in need of reforms to ensure control. He instituted educational classes after finding out that 157 inmates could neither read nor write. He cleaned up and reorganized the hospital staff to ensure immediate medical attention for the prisoners. He instituted the nation's first prison cafeteria system to provide hot food and a larger selection. A commissary department was introduced so that inmates could buy small things with the money they'd earned. He bought secondhand barber chairs in Chicago and turned a large unused room into a formal and sanitary barbershop for the inmates.

On April 28, 1930, newspapers announced that the warden of the state prison had a plan to stop unrest. Psychology, distributed by radio, was the instrument that would be used by Warden Henry C. Hill to fend off the unrest that had caused a series of rebellions in other prisons. "Back of it is a corps of straight-shooting guards.…The radio has two purposes: Through loudspeakers in the cell houses it gives the prisoners for about two hours daily the baseball scores, music and the like. It also gives the warden a chance to voice his ideas on prison behavior."

"A short time after the radio was installed, I made my first broadcast to the prisoners," said Warden Hill. "I told them that I would try to make the Illinois penitentiary as good a place as possible for them to serve their time provided they would reciprocate by behaving. At the same time, I warned that punishment for misconduct would be more severe than under the previous administration."

Every week, Warden Hill went on the air, telling the prisoners the advantages of serving their time in an orderly manner and emphasizing that those who might happen to escape would be constantly harassed by fear of recapture. The prison cafeteria was instituted as the only system by which prisoners could obtain their food hot; the barbershop, where twenty-five student barbers were being trained, was founded as a sanitary measure. Both these and the radio elicited hundreds of appreciative letters from prisoners, the warden said. Warden Hill admitted that he had no illusions regarding the docility of all his prisoners. He instructed all guards to go to target practice regularly and to become crack shots.

SMOKING RIGHTS

On October 7, 1929, the newspaper read: "Congressmen who vote dry and drink wet aren't hypocrites, but 'practical politicians;' that right on the heels of the railroads doing away with the non-smoking rules in their diners, the women of Joliet prison have been given smoking rights equal with the men inmates."

3

JOLIET PRISON IN THE NEWS 1930-39

CIVIL SERVICE EXAMINATIONS

On April 29, 1930, new guards were on duty at Illinois state prisons at Joliet-Stateville, Chester and Pontiac as a result of civil service examinations held earlier that month to weed out weak links in the state's penal system and to strengthen the morale of prison forces. Old guards who were not able to pass the test were replaced in most instances by World War I veterans.

CLYDE STRATTON

On February 17, 1930, Clyde Stratton was arrested for a burglary that netted him only a few dollars' worth of loot. But then it was discovered that he was a notorious murderer who'd been convicted of murdering J. L. Crowder, Silvis banker, in 1912. Crowder died four months after a gang of bandits led by Stratton held him up one Saturday night, and after beating him severely, they made away with about $900. It was decided that Stratton should be charged as a habitual criminal. Conviction on that charge meant life imprisonment. He was fifty-two years old and broken and old beyond his years. While awaiting trial, Stratton attempted to lead a jail break from the Will County jail. Once that might have been an easy trick for him, for he boasted escapes from fifty-one jails and prisons when he was incarcerated in Rock Island. He escaped from the Rock Island County jail, leading twelve men to freedom by way of a skylight, but he was recaptured at once. He escaped from Joliet Penitentiary during his sentence from Rock Island County but was recaptured in Ohio, and after serving an unfinished term in an Ohio prison, he came back to Joliet and finished his murder term of fourteen years.

A CONVICT INVENTOR

In 1930, it was reported that John King, an aged convict, had invented an airplane propeller of revolutionary design. He refused all monetary offers for his invention, insisting that when society released him from prison, it would receive the benefits of his discovery. Though King had been incarcerated for fifteen years and had never seen a modern airplane, the United States Navy, Henry Ford and the Guggenheim Foundation communicated with him about the propeller. The original idea for his invention came in a dream while he was in solitary confinement. He worked for five years on the plans.

After Henry Hill became warden of the state penitentiary, King was permitted the use of the prison workshop to complete the model. His discovery was a multiple propeller designed to use every ounce of horsepower, giving 90 percent efficiency instead of 40 percent, as in the present types. There are four blades, each connected separately to a hollow central shaft. As the outer shaft revolves, the blades move back and forth along the length of the shaft. At maximum speed, each blade makes one thousand trips in a minute, feathering automatically in the direction of flight and changing to the proper drawing pitch at the point of maximum pull.

LUCILLE TINCHER

On November 25, 1930, Lucille Tincher was arrested for aiding and abetting three bank robbers in their escape from the Olney jail. She and Agnes Kelly pleaded guilty, and they were each sentenced to serve one year to life in the women's prison at Joliet.

THE 1931 PRISON RIOT

On February 22, 1931, three prisoners attempted a prison break and were shot to death when they attempted to scale the walls. The news reports said that prison guards had been forewarned of the plot. The guards, armed with powerful searchlights and machine guns, found the three men easy targets and "mowed them down before they had a chance to reach two automobiles parked on the roadside near the prison." The occupants of the cars, pursued by guards in two automobiles, drove rapidly toward Chicago and escaped.

A week later, Joseph Oakley died after being in solitary confinement for insubordination. He was shackled, as was the customary punishment, with his wrists cuffed to the bars above his head for three days before he died. A coroner's jury absolved prison officials of blame for the death. It was ruled that he died from a blood clot, but the state legislature directed a committee to visit the penitentiary and make an investigation. This action, along with articles and editorials that they'd read in the newspapers, led convicts to believe that public sympathy was with them.

There had been growing discontent among the convicts at Joliet's old state penitentiary. Newspapers published editorials about alleged conditions in the prison, and the state legislature appointed an investigating committee. Prisoners were freely discussing the events as portrayed in the articles. Prison administration began preparing for a revolt.

Violence broke out at noon on Saturday, March 14. The trouble started with prisoners booing and getting up from their places at the tables in the dining hall. Warden Hill was notified and sent Deputy Wardens George Erickson and Frank Kness to the dining hall. The men wouldn't let them in. Erickson and Kness reported back to Warden Hill, who called for reinforcements. The guards, who were usually not allowed to carry firearms, hurried to the prison armory.

The 1,100 convicts refused to march to their cells and instead milled about the hall. They smashed dishes and tables, battered the pans from which their food was served. Most of them surged into the prison yard. Others smashed equipment and windowpanes in the chair factory.

Within a few minutes, the outer walls were manned by machine gunners. Warning shots fired from the walls sent inmates running for cover; about sixty of them ran for the kitchen. Leaving it thoroughly wrecked, they went on to the dining hall, smashing furniture, tearing tables and chairs from the concrete floor and hurling them through windows. Three of the rioting prisoners were felled by sharpshooting guards on the high, castellated wall, picked off one by one as they attacked a captain of prison guards at the door of the dining hall. Captain B.A. Davenport suffered a broken arm. Two fiber furniture shops were demolished, and fire was started in one cell house. It was quickly extinguished, as the limestone cell blocks were virtually fireproof.

Some convicts were herded back to their cells. Hidden sentry boxes with rifle slots had been installed recently at the end of each corridor. Sentries hidden in the concealed posts fired warning shots and tossed tear gas bombs to drive the unruly prisoners into their cells. One convict was wounded when struck by a ricocheting bullet fired into the air.

City and highway police surrounded the old stone prison, armed with shotguns, rifles and revolvers. None of the prisoners were armed, and there was no attempt to escape. "They thought today was a good day to take over the prison," said the warden. Forty-three ringleaders were locked up that night in solitary confinement, with irons on their hands and feet.

It was feared that the revolt would spread to the new Stateville prison three miles north of Joliet on the west side of the Des Plaines River. That Saturday night, six steel saws were found in a cell there. A joint riot and attempted jail break had apparently been interrupted. A coded message telling of an automobile to be ready for the plotters led to the discovery.

Monday morning, Warden Hill announced to newspapermen at the old penitentiary that a second of the wounded inmates had died. George Jakowanis was the sixth death in three weeks to require a coroner's inquiry. Hill then gave a statement asserting that Reverend Whitmeyer had been asked to resign three weeks before, after the discovery of evidence that he had been instigating unrest and carrying letters to and from prisoners. "I have these letters," he assured them. His resignation was received on February 25, three days after the fatal ambush of three escaping prisoners whose deaths he called "murder" at the hands of prison guards. Whitmeyer was "obstructing justice by advising the convicts not to talk." Warden Hill was asked to comment on the chaplain's note of resignation, in which he had expressed the kindliest feelings toward the warden. "He ought to have kindly feelings toward me," Hill said. "I have talked to him as a father. I have done everything I could to get him to abide by the prison rules."

The warden and his aides continued to supervise the reorganization with the greatest possible caution. Hill was fearful that if the prisoners were kept in their cells on short rations, they might cause further trouble. Warden Hill hoped to direct prison routine back into customary lines early in the week, but the death of the second convict was expected to cause further unrest among the prisoners. The forty-three ringleaders would be kept in solitary confinement indefinitely.

The convicts complained that the pardon board showed no respect for their relatives at pardon hearings; that a board of ten men passed on paroles, although only three actually heard the cases; that prisoners were not allowed more than one or two minutes to state their cases; and that parole applications were not given proper consideration. Six hundred prisoners sentenced under the old ten-year-to-life law for "robbery with a gun" had been discriminated against because the legislature had since changed the term to one year to life.

National guardsmen in northern Illinois were under orders to be ready for an emergency call to guard the Joliet Penitentiary if the disturbance got out of the control of officials there. One battalion of the 129th Infantry, whose personnel is drawn from within fifty miles of Joliet and Pontiac, was ordered to be ready to move on one hour's notice. Chicago guardsmen had been under orders to stand by since Saturday night.

Wednesday morning, the riot erupted at Stateville. Only the regular prison guards were kept that night at the old prison, but the number on duty was doubled. Companies E and G, whose members slept in the Joliet armory, would guard the old prison dining room the next morning.

The resulting damage was estimated to be $1 million. Only charred ruins remained of six of the seven buildings. The fire in the seventh, the machine shop, would not be fully extinguished until early Thursday. The work of rebuilding the mess hall would begin immediately, but orders were that the men be fed in their cells until all signs of mutiny had passed. Warden Hill was haggard and pale from lack of sleep and pain from a surgical incision that parted under the strain of quelling three outbreaks in five days.

Thursday, an ominous silence hung over the prison. Every prisoner was locked in his cell. Warden Henry C. Hill ordered that they be kept there—in isolation, with no privileges. More than six hundred armed guards—national guardsmen and city, state and county police—patrolled the prison, inside and out.

The matron in charge of the women prisoners, Bertha Finnegan, reported to Warden Hill that the women were also threatening an outbreak. Across the street, 145 women were housed in the women's prison. They were currently out of their cells, and it would be difficult to manage the women if things turned violent, especially without the use of clubs or guns. "The matron refused an offer of additional guards but carried 24 tear gas bombs across the street to throw at the women in case they rose." Warden Hill said the male prisoners had been encouraging the women to riot by signals flashed with handkerchiefs, lights and other prison systems of communication. Chief Walter Moody of the state highway police marched fifty of his men through the women's quarters as a demonstration.

By noon, they had recovered an assortment of knives and saws, as well as a miniature armory in the cell of a lifer—proof that further rioting and bloodshed was planned, asserted Warden Hill. He ordered Cook County Jail to not send a shipment of forty prisoners that was planned. There was no room for them in the old prison. It was the first time in the history of the institution that it refused to receive prisoners. Forty prisoners who were being sent to the new prison in anticipation of the arrival were instead returned to the old penitentiary.

On Friday, March 20, Warden Hill was the first witness before the investigation committee. Overcrowding of men in both prisons and resentment against parole board procedure were blamed for the prison outbreaks. Other sparks that helped touch off the revolt were the killing of three prisoners on February 22 as they tried to escape from the old building. The death of the prisoner in solitary confinement was the final straw.

Father Eligius Weir spoke next. The young, soft-spoken Catholic chaplain was a member of the Franciscan order. He testified that there were innocent men in the prison. He claimed that in thirty-five thousand personal interviews in the last four and a half years, at least five thousand of them had been complaints against the parole board. But he tempered this by saying that he had not attended meetings of the board and had learned what he related "from the boys." He was clearly a staunch supporter of Warden Hill, saying that the prisoners had been well treated. He felt that the trouble lay in the state's system of indeterminate sentences rather than with officials: "Neither the parole law nor parole regulations are at fault. It is the parole board members. Their attitude here has caused the trouble. There are boys of 16 here with hardened criminals. And at the state reformatory, built for wayward youths, there are men of 30, and there are insane criminals here who should be in the asylum for the criminal insane at Menard."

Chaplain Courageous

Chaplain "Buck" Weir served for 21 years as Joliet chaplain. He helped to quell riots, convert tough hoodlums into docile trustees, and thwart prison breaks. The kindly, courageous priest had earned the reputation of being the "toughest" man in the prison. "If they ever jab a knife in your back," the warden once warned him, "and march you to the gates and demand of the guard their freedom or your life, you must be prepared to be sacrificed. For the gates will not open." To such warnings, Father Weir paid little heed. During the 1931 Joliet riots—called by experts the worst in history—he was the only official to remain inside the prison amid a horde of raging

Chaplain Courageous. "In the 21 Years that Father Eligius Weir Served as Joliet's Chaplain, he was known as the kindest, yet 'toughest' man in the prison." San Francisco Examiner, *January 16, 1949.*

convicts. While others fled outside, he stayed behind to try to calm more than 4,000 men bent on murder and destruction.

—*Charles Renshaw Jr., 1949*

THE WOMEN MOVE TO DWIGHT

On April 9, 1931, it was announced that a new security cottage at the women's reformatory near Dwight was discussed at a meeting of the reformatory board. Estimated to cost between $75,000 and $100,000, the cottage would take care of the inmates of the women's prison at Joliet. There were then 136 women in the Joliet institution, which it proposed to abandon.

SHERIFF TAKES SHALLBERG TO JOLIET PRISON

Robert C. Shallberg, former vice president and cashier of the People's Savings Bank and Trust company of Moline, became a prisoner in the Illinois State Penitentiary on June 17, 1931. Sheriff Fred Schlueter transferred Shallberg to prison by automobile, leaving Rock Island at eight o'clock in the morning.

They were accompanied by a friend of the sheriff, who served as a guard, and Newton Gerhradt, who was returned to the penitentiary for violating a parole on a larceny charge. Shallberg began serving three consecutive sentences of one to ten years each for embezzlement.

Stolen Suit

On July 4, 1931, Arthur A. Miller walked out of the prison in a collegiate-cut gray suit owned by the warden's son. The trusted convict had dieted for two months to reduce his waistline so that young Hill's clothing would fit him. He had also taken one of the son's best golf clubs with him as an added touch. Miller entered the prison twelve years before to serve a life sentence. Since becoming a trustee several years before, he had been allowed access to Warden Hill's quarters as his personal barber. Selecting Independence Day for his walk to freedom, Miller went into the warden's home as if about on his duties. He donned silk underwear, socks, a white shirt, a blue tie, shoes, a suit and a panama hat, which Hill's son had laid out. Then he picked up the golf club and walked across the prison yard, clipping off a dandelion occasionally. He nodded cheerfully to guards at the penitentiary gate, and, thinking he was a visitor, they let him out.

A New Dormitory

On September 19, 1931, it was announced that construction would soon begin on a new addition to the state penitentiary at Joliet. The new project, to comprise five single-story dormitories, a central kitchen and a dining room, would be built on a plot east of the women's prison, about eight hundred yards from the edge of the now abandoned quarry at the old penitentiary. The plan of construction was unique in that there would be no walls or cellblocks. Inmates would sleep in open halls with barred windows and doors as the only safeguards against escape. Surrounding the prison yard would be two barbed-wire fences, the first about twenty feet from the buildings and the second about sixty feet farther away. Only first-term inmates showing a tractable disposition would be housed in the new dormitories. On a European junket for study of foreign methods of penology, the prison commission acquired the theory that segregation of first offenders is a prime necessity in prison reform.

JOLIET BOUND BY KANSAS JOE MCCOY
AND MEMPHIS MINNIE

This song was later performed by John Mellencamp, Rory Block, Wynton Marsalis and Eric Clapton.

Now the police coming; With his ball and chain—Mmmm mmmm
Police coming; With his ball and chain
And they accusing me of murder; Never harmed a man

Now some got six months; Some got a solid year—Mmmm mmmm
Some got six months; Some got one solid year
Now I mean my buddy; Got a lifetime here

Now the judge he pleaded; Clerk, he wrote it down—Mmmm mmmm
Judge he pleaded; Clerk, he wrote it down
That if I miss jail sentence now; Must be Joliet Bound

Now cook my supper; Let me go to bed—Mmmm mmmm
Cook my supper now; Let me go to bed
I've been drinking white lightning; And it's gone to my head

Now quit me baby; Do anything you want to do—Mmmm mmmm
Quit me baby; Do anything you want to do
Some day you gonna want me; Cinch and I won't want you

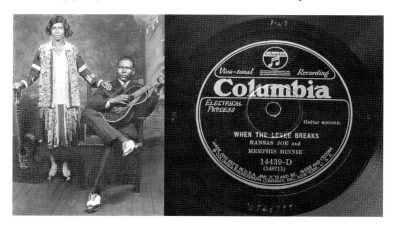

Memphis Minnie and her first husband/accompanist, Kansas Joe McCoy.
Cover of When the Levee Breaks, *1929.*

93

Now the police shoved (shivved) his old; Pistol in my side—Mmmm mmmm
Police shoved his old; Pistol in my side
Says, if you run big boy, now; Must be born to die

When they had my trial; You could not be found—Mmmm mmmm
Had my trial; You could not be found
Now and I got all messed up; And I'm Joliet Bound

AUTO LICENSE TAGS

On October 28, 1931, it was announced that auto license tags would be made at Joliet. Under the provisions of this law, the penal institutions were to begin the manufacture of soap (Joliet), knitted underwear (Chester), automobile license tags and other sheet metal articles (Stateville). The cost of the license tags, together with the envelopes in which they were mailed and copies of the motor vehicle laws of the state, would amount to about $7.50 per one hundred pairs. Director Brandon estimated the output of tags to approach twenty thousand each day. The printing business would remain at Pontiac and furniture at Joliet, while cement would be made at all prisons.

BABY FACE NELSON

Lester M. Gillis was first arrested at the age of thirteen and was sent to reform school. He completed his third incarceration at St. Charles Reformatory and was paroled on July 11, 1926. There, he exhibited such good behavior that the school superintendent made him a college captain—a sort of monitor with authority over seventy-five boys. He was married two years later, at the age of twenty, to Helen Wawzynak, a department store salesgirl. They had two children, a son and a daughter. Shortly after, he turned his attention to robbing banks. In 1931, police began noticing a man called George Nelson. Investigating further, they learned that he was known to his associates as "Baby Face." It didn't take them long to discover that Baby Face Nelson had earlier gone by the name Lester Gillis.

In February 1931, Nelson was arrested with several other men as an alleged bank robber. In July, he was convicted of robbing the Hillside State

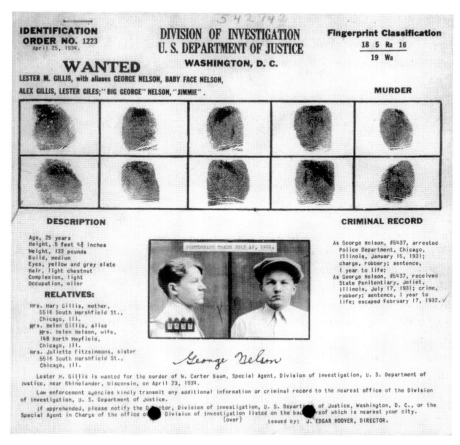

Baby Face Nelson. *Justice Department File, 1934.*

Bank of $4,155 and sentenced to Joliet Penitentiary for a term of one year to life. In February 1932, he was removed from prison to stand trial at Wheaton on a charge of robbing the Itasca State Bank of $4,000. That night, after being formally sentenced, he was placed into the custody of a Joliet prison guard who would take him back to prison. Alighting from their train in the city of Joliet, the guard and the prisoner boarded a taxi. Nelson was handcuffed to Martin. As they approached the high prison gates in their cab, Nelson suddenly pressed a revolver against Martin's side. Martin opened the handcuffs, as directed, and Nelson disarmed him. He then ordered the chauffeur to drive to a cemetery near Summit, a suburb of Chicago. There, he put the driver and the guard out of the cab and drove away. It was not discovered how Nelson got the gun.

Nelson became a "trigger man" for a rumrunning gang operating in California near San Francisco. After John Dillinger's toy gun escape from the county jail at Crown Point, Indiana, in early March, 1934, it was apparent that Nelson had become part of Dillinger's gang.

On April 22, a trap was laid for Dillinger at Little Bohemia, near Rhinelander, Wisconsin. Federal Agent W. Carter Baum thought he recognized a man sitting in an automobile as a farmer of the district. When Baum and a constable approached the machine, Nelson recognized them as officers and opened fire. Baum was shot through the neck and killed. Jay Newman, another agent, and the constable were critically wounded. Nelson's trigger finger apparently aided Dillinger and the other members of the mob to escape.

Dillinger was killed in Chicago on July 22. It seemed that Nelson was the apparent successor to the slain czar of American criminals. In August 1934, Nelson was designated by the Department of Justice as the new U.S. Public Enemy Number One. Nelson's next appearance was in Barrington, a Chicago suburb, where on November 27, he and a companion shot to death two federal agents. Nelson received his fatal wounds in that gun battle. Nelson was dumped into a prairie grave fifteen miles from the site of the gun battle; his companions had abandoned him.

A LUCKY PENNY

In 1932, Warden Hill accepted a promotion to head up the federal prison at Lewisburg, Pennsylvania. As he left, a prison guard gave him a gift of an 1833 penny. The guard told Hill that he wanted him to have the coin that he'd carried for over thirty-two years as a good luck piece, saying, "It may serve you well in the future." Hill left Galesburg for his next assignment. When he was near Leland, Illinois, his vehicle was crowded off the road and flipped end over end three times. Hill had to crawl out of the car that was upside down. He was miraculously unhurt. Tom Wilson wrote in 2010, "When Warden Hill collected himself, he found his watch, pencil, rifle, shotgun and baggage were strewn around the area. One item that remained on his person was the 1833 penny given to him as a good-luck gift from the Joliet prison guard. Henry Hill told friends in Galesburg that it appeared the intended lucky coin had indeed served him well."

MYSTERIOUS TENOR VOICE
HEARD IN PRISON CEMETERY

On July 26, 1932, it was reported that every night around midnight, a high-pitched and clear tenor voice could be heard chanting songs in Latin from the potter's field, the burial place of convicts who died in the Illinois State Penitentiary. Hundreds of people were staying all night in the bleak and gloomy cemetery, hoping to hear the voice. The graveyard, unused for three years, was located on the summit of Monkey Hill in a desolate region half a mile from the women's penitentiary. After this article ran, a crowd of two thousand curious men and women gathered to hear the mournful chant. They were disappointed that the voice was silent. It was revealed that the voice belonged to William Chrysler, a convict trustee. It was his duty to go to the quarry during the night and morning and shut off the pumps. He had to make three or four trips each night and morning and to do so passed about four hundred yards from the cemetery. He entertained himself on these walks by bursting into song.

A TOUR OF THE PRISON

On October 20, 1932, the third district of the Illinois Federation of Women's Clubs (which included a group from the Calumet City Women's Club) enjoyed a tour of unusual interest through the women's quarters of the Joliet Prison. About five hundred people were included in the party, of which thirty-four were members of the local club. Following the dinner, which was served at the institution, the group toured the prison under the direction of Mrs. Finnegan, the matron, and Mr. Whipp, the superintendent of the Illinois institution. The women also heard a fine talk from the doctor who was in charge of the quarters. This instructive trip was greatly enjoyed by the women who were in attendance.

HEAD OF JOLIET WOMEN'S PRISON

On November 16, 1932, it was announced that Helen H. Hazard, former Rock Island schoolteacher, would replace Bertha Finnegan as the head of Joliet Women's Prison. She was assigned to the office of the parole board in Chicago and would also continue as superintendent of the Illinois women's reformatory at Dwight. This arrangement would be until the first of the new year, when the women prisoners at Joliet would be transferred to Dwight. Hazard had previously studied in Europe and served in executive capacities at the women's reformatory at Niantic, Connecticut, and the federal prison for women at Alderson, West Virginia.

SEGREGATION OF MENTALLY ILL PATIENTS

Segregation of mentally ill offenders was urged before a session of the Illinois legislature as a pressing measure for protection of society. At a conference of criminologists, psychiatrists and social workers held at the criminal court building on December 17, 1932, Dr. Harry R. Hoffman, director of the court behavior clinic, was instructed to appoint a committee of nine to work out a plan for submission to Governor-Elect Henry Horner for presentation to the assembly.

The proposed measure was to provide for the incarceration of delinquents who were mentally ill and deemed a danger to society. Dr. Hoffman, opening the session, declared the problem of handling feebleminded delinquents was one of the most serious now confronting the people of Illinois. The meeting followed close on the sentencing to the electric chair of James "Iggy" Varecha, a former inmate of the state hospital at Dixon, who killed one man and raped several women. Under a segregation system, it was pointed out, Varecha would not have been running at large. Warden Whipp said that the women's prison at Joliet, which accommodated about 350, was now empty since the women had been removed to Dwight and that it could be used in beginning a new system of segregation without new cost, if the legislature passed the requisite bills.

DISCIPLINE IN THE JOLIET PRISONS

On December 23, 1932, the *Chicago Tribune* continued a series of prison articles with a report by Willard Edwards on discipline in the Joliet prisons. In this second article, the life of the convicts at the old prison, on the honor farm and in the women's prison was described:

> *The gruff tones of a drill sergeant rend the wintry air in the yard of the old Joliet prison. The measured tread of marching feet on the frozen ground echoes*

against the yellow stone walls. "Column right!" yells the leader. The marching convicts, four abreast, in faded blue and brown uniforms, swing sharply. The man who has given the order takes up the marching count. "One-two-three-four!" he barks in the singsong army chant. First Assistant Warden Edward M. Stubblefield, in charge of the old prison, looks on critically. His keen eyes watch for any deviation from the brisk, military stride. Finally satisfied, he turns away. The clump-clump of hobnailed shoes continues.

There is no Christmas cheer evident in the old prison. There are no sauntering convicts, cigarette in mouth, as at Stateville. Here are gathered together the incorrigibles, the old timers, the riffraff, the scum of the underworld of Chicago and other Illinois cities, who resent their captivity and show it. This is the type of men, the next governor of Illinois points out, for whom the penal laws of the state must be revised with a view to making them more effective against the organized and habitual criminal.

Not many of the men in the old prison could give "clear evidence of their fitness for a life of freedom," Assistant Warden Stubblefield asserts. An iron hand is needed to rule them and keep them from mutiny. Many times in the last fifty years blood has been shed here by rioting convicts. They have been kept under control now since Stubblefield took charge in the summer of 1931 after the riots which resulted in the slaying of three convicts.

When the new prison at Stateville was built eight years ago a system was inaugurated whereby prisoners were rewarded for good behavior by a transfer to the modern institution with its airy, sunlit cells, its less stringent regulations. The result has been the gradual accumulation in the old prison of the more hardened criminals, who find it impossible to behave if given any privileges.

Strangely enough, many of the long termers prefer incarceration at the old prison, Stubblefield reveals. In the first place, they dislike the association with the younger prisoners, whom they refer to contemptuously as "punks." Secondly, they are uneasy under the rather easy regime prevalent at Stateville. They want to be with their own kind and they want to be handled without gloves. There is no desire for reform in them and they are irritated at the efforts of the state to improve them. "I have sent some of the old-timers to Stateville as a reward for good behavior and have had them plead after a few weeks there to be returned to the old prison," says Stubblefield. He too has the same great problem of idleness to combat that exists at Stateville. He has solved it partly by inaugurating a system of calisthenics and drilling, which keeps the men's bodies healthy and their minds occupied for portions of the day. "I've opened a gymnasium where forty to fifty boxers get training each day," Stubblefield remarks, "The drilling and the calisthenics also do some good. These men need more strict discipline and they get it. They wouldn't understand privileges. Marching in the yard, under the supervision of an inmate who acts as sergeant, is the sort of rigorous exercise which they prefer. We have only fifteen acres here to take care of 1,759 prisoners. We have more than one-half the number of inmates at Stateville and less than one-fourth the area in which to take care of them. Smoking by inmates is allowed only in the cells. The guards are on the job all the time. Guards are not permitted to smoke while on duty and their coats must be buttoned up and their demeanor strictly business-like at all times. Silence is enforced in the yard and in the dining room."

Stubblefield looks forward to the completion of a blanket factory, now being constructed, to help keep the men busy. This factory will supply blankets, uniforms, and other articles of woolen clothing for all state institutions.

"We have a merit system and the reward is time off for good behavior," says Stubblefield. "That is the only reward these men appreciate and want. When a prisoner is admitted, he is put in grade C. After three months of good behavior he is put in Grade B and three months more of good behavior gets him in Grade A. In the last grade, of course, he gets more days off for good behavior and he is not allowed to see the parole board until he is Grade A. After a man is in the old prison a year and has seen the parole board, he can be transferred to Stateville. If his behavior is bad there, he is sent back to the old prison."

After inspecting the old prison with its rigorous discipline, the visitor was startled by what he saw when he motored west of Stateville to the headquarters of the honor farm. A small group of barns and other farm buildings surround a red brick structure, which resembles a college dormitory. In the barnyard are overalled prisoners working without supervision. All over the 2,200 acres of the farm are other prisoners, also unguarded. Prisoners were scrubbing the floors of the kitchen. An appetizing odor came from the cooking vessels. In a big lounging room, prisoners listened to the radio, read magazines, or talked together. Upstairs, in comfortable bedrooms, others reclined. There are seven guards assigned to handle the 117 honor prisoners, but the warden and reporter saw not one of them during an hour's visit. The entire contingent of prisoners could walk off the farm, disappear into the cornfields, and their absence might not be noticed for hours.

Escapes have been frequent in the past from the honor farm, but the reporter had a feeling that they will be few this winter. Not many prisoners could find better lodging in the outside world than this comfortable country home.

The women's prison is the fourth penal institution at Joliet. Situated near the old prison, the number of its inmates is rapidly decreasing, as prisoners are transferred to the new women's prison at Dwight. Only sixty now remain.

JOLIET PRISON SCHOOL

In 1933, Richard Loeb became the Joliet Prison School headmaster. The faculty included Edward "the Society Bandit" Dillon, who taught English; lawyer/kidnapper Joseph Pursifull, who taught Latin; and a Chicago forger named Mark Oettinger, who taught math.

COOK COUNTY'S WAR AGAINST CRIME

On October 31, 1933, it was noted that a record 11,500 felons in Illinois prisons was a new record. The cause for these conditions was largely Cook County's crime war. Five hundred persons had been sentenced in Chicago courts, and most of them were already dispatched to penitentiaries, since the campaign against criminals had begun approximately three months before. Warden Frank D. Whipp estimated that the two institutions at Joliet could accommodate another two hundred prisoners. He remarked, "We're crowded. But you can always shove another passenger into a crowded streetcar."

ROGER TOUHY

On February 25, 1934, Roger Touhy and two of his gangsters were "taken for a ride"—forty miles to Joliet Prison to begin penitentiary sentences that will end in the year 2033. The three—Touhy, once head of a powerful gang; Albert Kator; and Gustav "Gloomy Gus" Shaefer—were delivered at the prison in handcuffs and leg irons. A parade of eleven squad cars, full of police and deputies armed with machine guns and riot guns, sped to Joliet with the prisoners at a fifty-mile-an-hour clip. Other cars patrolled the road ahead. Traffic was stopped at all crossroads, giving the gangsters a "clear board" for a fast trip to jail. The caravan set out thirty-six hours after a jury convicted the three of the $70,000 kidnapping of John "Jake" Factor. Touhy,

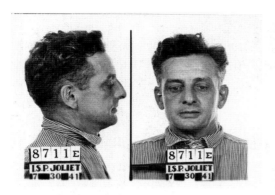

Roger Touhy, July 30, 1941. *The Mob Museum.*

who stood weak and nervous to hear the sentence pronounced, was in tears when the parade arrived at the prison. Once inside the gates, Touhy, the "big shot" of a gang that allegedly split the Chicago territory with the Capone gang, became no. 8711. Within an hour, they were photographed, bathed, shaved and in prison uniforms.

DR. ALICE WYNEKOOP

On March 6, 1934, a jury found Dr. Alice Lindsay Wynekoop guilty of the murder of her twenty-three-year-old daughter-in-law, Rheta Gardner Wynekoop. The unhappy woman was married to the doctor's son Earle. She was chloroformed and shot while in the doctor's care. The doctor confessed to the murder but later retracted her confession. There were many theories—that she was covering for her son, that the suicidal victim had someone's help in trying to end her life, that Earle had hired someone to kill his wife—but the mystery remained. Dr. Wynekoop was one of Chicago's most admired and respected physicians. At sixty-three years old, she was said to be in critical health. The jury had deliberated for one hour and thirty-six minutes before finding her guilty. The penalty was fixed at twenty-five years imprisonment. Walker, elder son of the defendant, declared that the verdict was a terrible shame. Dr. Catherine Wynekoop, brilliant young daughter of the convicted woman, was overcome and declined to comment. Prosecutor Charles S. Dougherty was elated but tired from the bitter legal battle. He said that he believed justice had been done. W.W. Smith, chief of counsel for the defense, immediately made a motion for a new trial. The date was set by Judge Miller for March 24. The second trial upheld her conviction, and she was taken to Joliet

Pictured in 1923   Dr. Alice L. Wynekoop as she appears today.   Pictured in 1915

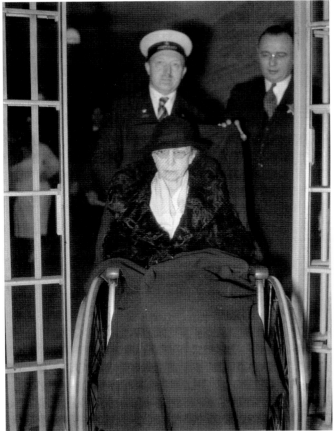

Above: Photographs and a pen drawing of Alice Wynekoop. Daily Advertiser, *Lafayette, Louisiana, December 11, 1933.*

Left: Alice Wynekoop in the courtroom, circa March 1934. *Chicago History Press.*

women's prison. She was released in December 1947. She maintained her innocence and in October 1948 submitted to a private lie detector test. The results showed that Dr. Wynekoop had not committed the crime and did not know who was responsible. She died in a nursing home on July 4, 1955, where she was living under an assumed name.

SYCAMORE ELKS GO TO PRISON

On June 28, 1934, the *De Kalb Daily Chronicle* reported on a baseball game that was planned between the Sycamore Elks team and a prisoners' team at the Joliet State Penitentiary. The game would be played at the prison because the "undergrads" there were not prone to take trips away from the "alma mater," and all athletic events had to be played on the home field. The manager of the Elks team said he would be glad to take his team down there provided he could be assured that none of them would have to remain there permanently.

The Elks were disappointed to learn that because of the crowded condition of the prison and because of troubles in the past that grew out of visits by strangers, it was not probable that the men would be permitted to go through the big plant.

THE LINDBERGH BABY KIDNAPPING

On July 21, 1934, a convict in the state prison at Joliet turned over to Warden Frank B. Whipp what he said was the "true story" of the Lindbergh baby kidnapping. He named Frank Nash, slain in the Kansas City union station massacre a year before, and Al Capone, then in the Cook County Jail in Chicago, as the men behind the plot. The convict, John Pawelczyk, said the kidnapping was planned to free Capone, following denial of his appeal from an income tax conviction. At the time of the kidnapping, Capone offered to aid authorities in finding the child and said he had "friends" who could trace the kidnappers. The information was turned over to federal authorities. Pawelczyk said he met Nash while both were at Leavenworth Prison. At that time, he and Nash communicated by means of a code that later appeared on a note left at the Lindbergh home. Pawelcyzk named as the actual kidnappers Nash, Bob Sandvich and a woman friend of the latter named only as "Tessie." Sandvich, he said,

Lindbergh baby kidnapping article "Crime of the Century," by Kent Allerton Hunter and Frank Gorman. *History.com*

killed the Lindbergh child with a blow over the head after a tire had blown out on their car, and they had become panic stricken. According to the convict's story, Capone conceived the plot in a desperate attempt to win his freedom. If that were true, detectives pointed out, the comparatively low ransom demand of $50,000, which puzzled authorities, might be explained. Pawelzyk, sentenced in Chicago, was serving a one- to ten-year term for manslaughter.

WARDEN JOSEPH RAGEN

In 1935, Joseph E. Ragen was named warden at both the Stateville and Joliet Prisons after the escape of Henry "Midget" Fernekes. He was later recognized by his contemporaries as the nation's best prison administrator. Ragen tackled the job of rehabilitating the old Joliet Prison. In the west cell house, 840 cells were modernized. These replaced the old cubicles without water or toilet facilities. The kitchen, dining room, ice plant and bakery adjoining the cell block were all rehabilitated at a cost of about $3.4 million. During the reconstruction, a lead key was found in an air duct. The key was used to free twenty-one men from their cells in an escape attempt. How this had been accomplished was a mystery for thirty years.

Both prisons were virtually self-sustaining. Clothing was made in a textile mill and tailor shop. Food for all prison inmates and several other state institutions was supplied by the prison's 2,200-acre farm. The 180 prisoner farmers did all of the work without modern machinery, as Ragen believed

Joseph Ragen was the topic of the 1957 biography *Warden Ragen of Joliet* by Gladys A. Erickson. *Joliet Area Historical Museum, Illinois.*

it necessary to create as much work as possible to keep the men busy. All prisoners under Ragen's administration were required to complete a grade school education in the prison schools, if they had not done so before being sentenced. They also had the opportunity to attend high school or any of the thirty-two vocational trade schools. By 1949, Ragen had been responsible for something like 17,600 prisoners. He was awarded the John Howard Association medal for outstanding work in rehabilitating prisoners.

A FALL FROM THE WALL

On April 29, 1935, four convicts made a daring break for freedom from the old Joliet Penitentiary, but three of them were back in cells that evening. The only one who was still at liberty was Edward Martin, thirty years old, who was serving a one- to twenty-year sentence for a 1929 robbery. Warden Frank D. Whipp said that Martin had served two previous prison terms and could be expected to put up a fight to avoid recapture. The first of the three convicts to be retaken was Arthur Schroeder, who was serving a one- to fourteen-year sentence for forgery from Will County. An hour after the escape, he was found in a field near the prison. Both of his ankles had been broken in a fall down the thirty-five-foot wall of the penitentiary. He weighed 272 pounds. George Patterson, forty-five, was sentenced from Williamson County in April 1934 for forgery. He was recaptured in a freight car near New Lenox, six miles east of Joliet. The last fugitive to be taken was William Kirkpatrick, thirty-three, who was sent to the prison from Peoria County in October 1931 for robbery. Kirkpatrick was found in a homeless camp two miles east of Joliet by a detail of prison guards under Captain J.R. Carpenter. He had sprained an ankle and could go no farther.

The escape of the four convicts was made at 2:20 a.m. from the diagnostic hospital section of the penitentiary, an enclosed area across the street from the main prison, which was formerly used as the women's prison. Since the women prisoners were transferred to Dwight, their former quarters were used for receiving new convicts who later were sent either to the old prison across the street or to the new prison at Stateville, two miles away.

Kirkpatrick, Martin, Patterson and Schroeder were detailed at the diagnostic hospital section as workers. They were quartered in a cell with Edward Kazda, a Chicago convict who had served eight years of a one- to ten-year larceny sentence. Schroeder, who worked in a boiler room, had secreted a wrench in the cell. When they were ready for the break, the four woke Kazda, but he refused to join them. They tied him up and put him in a closet. With the wrench, they pried bars off the cell window, then climbed a fire escape to a room from which they were able to jump to the prison wall. Securing a length of sash cord to the top of the wall, Patterson went down safely. Kirkpatrick sprained his ankle in landing, and the cord broke with Schroeder. Martin slid down a pipe.

AN INNOCENCE PROJECT

On July 15, 1935, four hoodlums—Bruno Austin, Alex Shapiro, Dave Sinnenberg and Morris Jacobs—swooped down on a blind pig, an illegal liquor store on Chicago's tough west side, intent on robbery. As they walked into the gangster-controlled joint, guns barked. Windows in the front of the place were shattered by revolver fire. Anthony Benidetto, an innocent bystander, fell dead. Two of the bandits were wounded. Then, as quickly as they had come, the men made their getaway. Picked up a few days later, they were charged with murder and robbery. At the trial, Vincenzo De Rosa, proprietor of the blind pig, testified that the only shots fired during the holdup had come from the guns of the four accused men. His son, Sam, stated he had been asleep throughout the incident. Explaining how two of the robbers could have been wounded if no one else had used a gun, witnesses said the men had shot each other. How the bandits could have blasted the windows when they had their backs turned toward them was not accounted for. In fixing punishment for the crime, the jury first voted eleven to one for the death penalty. Eventually, however, the men were given twelve years for robbery and life sentences for murder. The two terms were to run concurrently. After the culprits had been in prison for some time, Bruno Austin became Father Weir's secretary. He convinced the priest that Sam De Rosa, not the accused men, had fired the shot that killed Benidetto. Father Weir, having received the men's assurance that they would continue the program of character reformation they had already begun, went to work on their behalf.

Pointing an accusing but kindly finger, he wrote to Sam De Rosa, urging him to confess. For a long time, De Rosa didn't answer, but the priest's letters followed him wherever he went. Finally, in 1945, he cracked. Writing to the chaplain, he admitted that he had fired the fatal shot in defense of his father's store. Then began a three-year legal battle to free the four men. During that fight, Father Weir and Chicago attorney Luis Kutner, who had agreed to handle the case without fee, ran head-on into gangland. Itching for revenge and afraid their rackets would again be encroached on if the convicts were released, underworld characters made threats of violence and death. These attempts at intimidation were unsuccessful. Armed with a signed affidavit from De Rosa telling his part in the shooting, Kutner and Father Weir were finally ready to present their case in court. When he had heard all of the evidence, federal judge Michael Igoe set the men free on writs of habeas corpus. "Judge," said Bruno Austin, speaking for the group, "you will not be disappointed in us."

Once freed, the four men made good on their promise. Shapiro became the manager of an automobile accessory business. Sinnenberg, backed by friends, bought a grocery store. Jacobs became an X-ray technician, and Austin went with Father Weir to the Alverna Retreat Home as the former chaplain's secretary. Father Weir, the priest who played such a vital role in freeing prisoners, insisted, "There is no credit due me, it is an obligation I owe to all men—black, white, Jew or gentile. Long ago I vowed to help him who can't help himself."

JILTED LOVER

Mandeville W. Zenge, captured as a suspect in the mutilation murder of Dr. Walter J. Bauer of Kirksville, Missouri, steadfastly denied any connection with the killing. Herald and Review, *Decatur, Illinois, August 3, 1935.*

On July 30, 1935, Dr. Walter J. Bauer was kidnapped from Ann Arbor, Michigan. The thirty-eight-year-old doctor was a teacher at a school of osteopathy in Kirksville, Missouri. He was in Ann Arbor for the summer, studying at the University of Michigan. Dr. Bauer was found the next morning, having been emasculated with a pocketknife. Two gas station attendants drove him to the hospital. Before dying of the injury, he told of being abducted by a fellow hotel lodger he knew as "E.L. Jones of Chicago," who forced him at gunpoint to drive to Chicago.

A cab driver turned over to police some bloodstained clothing left behind by a passenger he had driven to Navy Pier at 10:45 p.m. the day before. Inside was a suicide note, written by Mandeville Zenge. Addressed to Zenge's

109

father, it said that because of his bitter feelings over Louise marrying that doctor, he was "going to end it all." Police soon discovered that Zenge and his childhood sweetheart, Louise Schaffer, had been engaged to be married for about seven years, when she broke it off. Shortly after, she married Dr. Bauer.

When Dr. Bauer's widow was shown the note, she sobbed, "They're both gone." Police captain John Stege called the note "a ruse" meant to throw the police off Zenge's track. An anonymous tip led to his arrest the next day. He steadfastly denied any involvement through over twenty hours of questioning. When shown a picture of Louise, he finally burst into tears. He admitted that he wrote the suicide note and demanded a lawyer.

The jury was out only four hours before pronouncing a verdict of guilty and a sentence of life in prison. Mandeville Zenge entered Joliet Prison on November 14, 1935. He would not be eligible for parole for twenty years. He died in Quincy, Illinois, in 1989.

EXECUTED

Mildred Hallmark's body was found in a ditch in a Peoria cemetery on June 17, 1935. Gerald Thompson was arrested after several girls revealed secretly to authorities that he had also attacked them. His diary included the names of sixteen girls who he had attacked, including Mildred Hallmark. He admitted that he had lured the girl into his automobile and beat her when

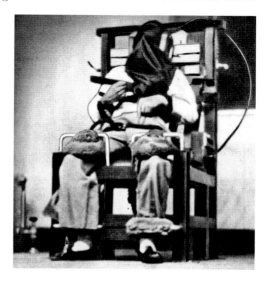

Gerald Thompson was strapped into "Old Smokey" on October 15, 1935. His last words were "I hope God will accept me." *David, Lester, "Mechanics of Killing,"* Mechanix Illustrated, *April 1948.*

she resisted his advances. When he was executed on October 15, 1935, her father was one of five hundred witnesses at the execution. Thompson had reportedly recently found faith in religion before his death.

SECRETARY TO TEN WARDENS

On November 4, 1935, Warden Joseph Ragen of the Joliet branch of the State Penitentiary announced the resignation of Alice H. Tindall. She had been secretary to ten wardens in her forty years of service. Her family had moved to Pontiac, Illinois, in 1868, and she began her career at the reformatory there. Her successor would be Harriet Hardy, who had been Ragen's secretary when he was in charge of the Menard prison.

DAYLIGHT BREAK FOR FREEDOM

On January 16, 1938, alert and sharpshooting guards were credited with foiling a daylight break for freedom of five long-term convicts from the state penitentiary at Joliet. Four of the men succeeded in scaling the twenty-two-foot prison wall. Two were stopped by bullets but were wounded only slightly. The others were captured as they attempted to flee toward the shelter of nearby buildings. The fifth man retreated to the prison proper when a guard began firing.

Ragen said the men, working in the prison laundry, overpowered a guard and tied him with sheets. They took his wallet, containing thirty-one dollars, but did not touch his gun. They bound together four short ladders used in the laundry and raced one hundred yards to the outer wall. Four of them got to the top of the wall. One sprained his ankle in jumping to the street and surrendered without struggle. Another ran into an officer of the prison force who was off duty. He also surrendered. Thomas Shaw, a tower guard, using a high-powered rifle, shot one of the men through the shoulder as he raced down the street. Another was wounded in the left leg as he made ready to jump from the wall. The last man heard the shooting and ran back to the laundry.

4

JOLIET PRISON IN THE NEWS 1940-69

HOLE OF CALCUTTA

In 1940, it was suggested that the Old Joliet Prison on Collins Street be abandoned. Former welfare director A.L. Bowen published his seven-year tenure report, which indicated that an expenditure of $10 million for permanent improvements at state welfare institutions was needed over the next four years. His report attacked the prison system in general for failure to reduce criminal conduct and rehabilitate criminals but called the state's penitentiary units, with the exception of the old prison at Joliet, "the most secure, the most sanitary, the best disciplined in the United States." Calling the Joliet institution's facilities and overcrowding "disgraceful, wasteful and inhumane," Bowen said the term "Hole of Calcutta" might be well applied to this old prison. He urged the abandonment of the structure.

GUN FIGHT VICTIM WAS ESCAPED CONVICT

The body of a man killed on December 6, 1940, in a gun fight in the railroad yards at Kansas City was identified by Joliet Prison officials as that of Roy Dowell, an escaped convict. Dowell entered the prison in 1923 from McLean County to serve three- to twenty-years for robbery. He escaped in 1927.

Two Police Killers Among 330 Felons Seeking Paroles

In May 1941, 330 parole applications of convicts from Cook County had been set for hearing on the June and July docket of the state parole board. One of them was Guy Van Tassel, who was considered one of Chicago's most dangerous criminals thirty-five years earlier. On November 19, 1906, Van Tassel shot and killed a policeman on his return from Hammond, Indiana, where he had blown a safe. Before that arrest, he had already spent thirteen years in prison for robbery and later tried twice to escape. Now sixty-eight years old, Van Tassel was seeking his release in order to return to his native Tennessee Hills.

Another candidate for parole was convicted cop killer Edward Morris. He turned from selling sausages to peddling whiskey. On January 3, 1921, policeman John Mullen was called to a speakeasy at Lincoln Avenue and Wells Street, where Morris was creating a disturbance. Morris drew a gun and ordered Mullen to raise his hands. As Mullen did so, Morris shot him in the back.

A third lifer, Edward Hettinger, was nineteen years old in November 1919, when he was sent to prison for the murder of Agnes Middleton. She was knocked unconscious by the burglar, who stole her jewelry and then slit her throat with a razor.

John Howe Jr. was making his first application for parole. The former state policeman was sentenced on May 14, 1940, to one year to life for a robbery committed in 1930. Originally committed to an asylum instead of prison, he escaped and through political influence was made a state policeman. Howe's old record was uncovered after his arrest as an alleged fixer of a jury that acquitted two Democratic politicians of voter fraud.

The Furnace Murderer

Rose Michaelis went missing on February 28, 1945. Her husband, Milton, returned from work in a war plant and found a heel of her shoe in the alley behind their apartment. When questioned by police, the building's janitor, thirty-one-year-old Joseph Nischt, gave "vague answers that sounded half-insane," according to Lieutenant Philip Breitzke of the homicide squad. Suddenly, the officer shouted, "What did you do with the body?" Nischt replied, "I put it in the furnace." He told of meeting Mrs. Michaelis in the alley and beating her with his fists. He said that he was drunk and didn't realize he knew the woman until he saw her on the ground. He then knew he had to get rid of her. He apologized to her family members when confronted, saying, "I'm sorry; I don't know why I did it."

On December 11, 1945, Joseph Nischt was sent to Joliet Prison to begin a life sentence. "Liquor did this to my boy," his father said. "I've learned he had 41 drinks of whiskey the night that woman was killed." Nischt was taken to prison from the county jail with seventeen other prisoners. After examination at the Joliet diagnostic depot, he was transferred to Stateville Penitentiary.

STEVENS HOTEL MURDER

In 1927, the Stevens Hotel opened on South Michigan Avenue in Chicago, covering the entire city block between Seventh and Eighth Streets. Called the "New Versailles," it had three thousand rooms and was the largest hotel in the world. It had restaurants, ballrooms, shops, a bowling alley and even a hospital. Guests could play miniature golf at the High-ho club on the roof. The once-opulent symbol of the Jazz Age was laid low by the Depression in the '30s, however. The hotel suffered a series of tragedies—the owners declared bankruptcy and were charged with financial corruption. One of them suffered a stroke, and the other died by suicide. Conrad Hilton later purchased the hotel, now known as Chicago Hilton and Towers.

On May 11, 1945, seventeen-year-old Morton Stein was found beaten and stabbed to death in a closet in room 733 of the Stevens Hotel. The victim had run away from home three months before. His father said that he had no idea where the boy had been or where he had gotten any money to live on. A companion who had registered for the room as Don Edwards was sought by police. The boys were described as wearing expensive clothes.

In September, Donald Jay Cook was arrested in Gretna, Louisiana, after he stole a car, and it was discovered that he was wanted in connection with the murder. He told FBI investigators that he met Stein at Montifiore school in April. Stein had committed two robberies—a bookie and a storekeeper. With the loot, the two boys went to New York and later returned to the Stevens Hotel in Chicago. Cook said that when he refused to help Stein with another robbery, Stein attacked him with a hunting knife. "I picked up a blackjack—both weapons were his—and hit him. The blackjack split. He still kept coming. I hit him with my fists. His knife dropped. We started struggling for it. Then he broke away from me and lunged. I grabbed the knife and struck." Cook boarded a bus bound for Texas hours before the body was discovered. He'd arrived in Dallas, where he'd stayed about three weeks and then moved on to New Orleans.

In October, Lieutenant Phil Breitzke of the Chicago Homicide Squad flew to New Orleans to bring Cook back. At the trial in December, fifteen-year-old "bobby socks girl" Shirley Allen took the witness stand. She calmly told of spending the day with Stein in the Stevens Hotel room on May 10. He told her that she'd have to visit him there, as he had a cold and was unable to leave the room. She denied that she'd been intimate with him. She said that she'd seen the blackjack and a push-button knife in the room, along with a book about the boys' idol, John Dillinger. Stein had once told her that he would avoid the mistakes that led to Dillinger's death at the hands of federal agents. She admitted that Stein was the dominating one of the two boys—that he carried a long-bladed knife in a holster, had threatened Cook with it during a quarrel and had lots of money. Cook had asked Stein for money and was given a dollar. He asked for more later and was refused. Allen left at 5:30 p.m.

In dispute of Cook's claim that he killed Stein in self-defense, the prosecution claimed that the murder happened during a quarrel over the division of the loot from several burglaries that both boys had committed. Thelia Stein, mother of the victim, took the stand, glaring at Cook throughout her testimony. She said that her son was "as good as the average boy." When it appeared that the self-defense plea wasn't going well, Cook changed his plea of not guilty of murder to guilty of manslaughter, for which the law provided a maximum penalty of fourteen years. Donald J. Cook was taken to Joliet in December 1945.

PETER LUNA

On June 17, 1946, Peter Luna, a seventeen-year-old convict from Hammond, Indiana, escaped from Joliet Prison. It was only two weeks after he had begun a one- to three-year term for stealing an automobile bumper and a flashlight. The boy escaped by climbing up a drainpipe to the roof of the prison diagnostic depot and walking down a fire escape to the street, where he stole a parked automobile and fled. He had been in a recreation yard with approximately 125 other convicts, Warden Joseph Ragen said. Several guards were on duty in the yard at the time, one of them less than one hundred feet from the drainpipe. Luna returned to prison after killing two bartenders in the Alamo Café later that year. He claimed self-defense but was convicted, serving fifteen and a half years before he died in the hospital at the Old Joliet Prison.

WHITE HEAT

Joliet was used for the exterior shots of the prison in the James Cagney film *White Heat* (1949), in which a psychopathic criminal makes a daring break from prison and leads his old gang in a payroll heist.

JAMES EARL RAY

In 1952, James Earl Ray served two years in Joliet for the armed robbery of a taxi driver. He was later sentenced to twenty years in the Missouri State Penitentiary for repeated offenses. In 1967, he escaped by hiding on a truck that was transporting bread from the prison bakery. On April 4, 1968, James Earl Ray murdered Dr. Martin Luther King Jr. at the Lorraine Motel in Memphis, Tennessee. He was arrested two months later at the London Heathrow Airport. The United Kingdom extradited him to Tennessee, where he pled guilty to avoid the death penalty. He was sentenced to ninety-nine years in prison. Three days later, he recanted his confession and began hinting at a larger conspiracy. He said that he had not personally killed Dr. King but might have been "partially responsible without knowing it." Ray also told an investigator that he purposefully left his weapon with fingerprints because he wanted to be a famous criminal. He believed he was too smart to be caught. Ray and six other convicts escaped from Brushy Mountain State Penitentiary in June 1977. They were recaptured three days later, and a year was added to Ray's sentence. Ray died in 1998 due to complications from Hepatitis C.

PAUL CRUMP

In 1953, Paul Crump was found guilty of the murder of Theodore P. Zukowski, a guard at Libby, McNeill & Libby food plant, during a $26,000 robbery. He was held at Cook County Jail for nine years and became a protector of sick and elderly inmates. While he was there, he published many poems and a novel, *Burn, Killer, Burn*. He won the support of Mahalia Jackson, Billy Graham and William Friedkin, a filmmaker who made a documentary about him. He escaped fifteen dates with the electric chair. Attorneys pleaded with the Illinois Parole and Pardon Board to spare his life on the grounds that during his years in prison he was rehabilitated. Crump's story became national news. The governor commuted the sentence to 199 years in prison. He arrived at the Illinois State Penitentiary Diagnostic Depot (at Joliet Penitentiary) the next Wednesday to undergo thirty days of physical and psychiatric tests. From there, he was sent to Pontiac, where he clashed with prison officials. He was transferred back to the Illinois Penitentiary at Joliet. There he worked in the clothing room and was permitted to read and write in his cell. He began experiencing psychotic episodes and spent the last seventeen years of his sentence at the Menard Psychiatric Center. He was finally released from prison on February 19, 1993. Adjustment was difficult. At sixty-two years old, Paul returned to a very different world than the one he had left.

JUSTICE

A television series called *Justice* was a dramatic show based on cases tried by lawyers of the legal aid society of New York City (1954–56). Episode twenty-two, "The Quiet Prisoner," features Joliet Prison.

BARRY COOK

Barry Z. Cook was a suspect in four unsolved Chicago murder cases in the late 1950s, including the "spyglass" murder of Margaret Gallagher in Lincoln Park. She was slain while sunbathing in the park. A man witnessed the crime through field glasses from a nearby apartment. He was also a suspect in the torso murder of fifteen-year-old high school student, Judith Mae Andersen, who was found stuffed into two oil drums in Montrose Harbor in August 1957; the mysterious deaths of the Grimes sisters; and the triple slayings of the Schuessler-Peterson boys. Although he was not convicted of any of these crimes, Cook was sentenced to the Illinois State Penitentiary on concurrent terms of one to fourteen years for seven charges of assault and one of assault to commit rape. He was shot and wounded by police when he tried to escape questioning about a series of rape attempts on the north side. He failed lie detector tests given in relation to two of the murders. Cook was twenty-five years old when he entered the Old Joliet Prison on July 2, 1958. Cook spent most of his time at Joliet working in the concrete shop where bricks are made, the textile shop and the machine shop. For a few months in 1959, he was transferred to the prison system's psychiatric division at Menard. In the spring of 1959, Cook was returned from Joliet and tried by a criminal court jury for the Gallagher murder. The jury returned a verdict of innocence. He was discharged on June 26, 1967, after serving almost nine years.

100ᵀᴴ BIRTHDAY

In 1958, the Old Joliet prison marked its 100th year. Warden Joseph Ragen joked that about the only thing that hadn't changed in the one hundred years since they opened a prison at Joliet is that timeless complaint: "Nobody likes it here." How did Joliet-Stateville celebrate its 100th birthday? "It's just another day," said Ragen. Then he chuckled, "I'll tell you one thing—we're not going to have an open house."

CAPTAIN ANDREW STASH

By 1959, Captain Andrew Stash had been in prison work for twenty-eight years. The Streator, Illinois native had been a senior guard captain at the penitentiary since 1953 and had for the last two years been in charge of the diagnostic depot or receiving station. His staff, including two lieutenants and twenty-five officers, was the first prison personnel to come in contact with the inmate as he entered the penitentiary. "We run the biggest little prison in the country, but every man who passes through our depot receives the same treatment, regardless of race, creed or color."

Captain Stash told a *Streator Times-Press* reporter: "We have no pets or friends here. These men are here to pay a debt to society and when they come to us all are treated equally." During their short three-to-six-week stay at the depot, the inmate is given individualized studies and examinations by trained sociologists, psychologists, and psychiatrists. The men are classified through their individual makeup, disposition and ability to respond to correctional treatment. Recommendations are then made to institution officials who decide where to assign them, either to Stateville, the Joliet branch or to Menard in Southern Illinois.

At the time the *Times-Press* reporter was at the diagnostic depot, Captain Stash had 172 prisoners registered, 21 for regular work details and 141 "fish" (new prisoners). Some of the men were going through classification sessions while others were attending indoctrination classes in which they become familiar with the rules and regulations of the new life ahead of them. Captain Stash said that in the indoctrination classes, every phase of the prison rehabilitation program is explained to the prisoner, who is told that he can learn a trade, take studies to complete his grade or high school education, and if he is interested, can acquire college correspondence courses for study in his cell. "We try to keep the prisoner occupied and working because idle men who have too much time to think about themselves cause trouble," Stash pointed out.

Stash started his career in prison work back in 1930. "It was just about the time of the depression and jobs were becoming scarce," Captain Stash recollected. "My boss at the steel mill said he would keep me on the payroll as long as he could but advised me to take the job at the penitentiary."

Most of Captain Stash's years at the prison were spent under Warden Ragen, recognized as one of the nation's outstanding penologists, and who was hailed for his "clean-up" at both branches of the state penitentiary. "In all my years of association with Warden Ragen, I've never asked for anything—promotions, or otherwise," Stash said. "Whatever I have received, he was responsible, because he is that type of man. If a person does his work, it doesn't go unnoticed by Mr. Ragen, who is not only fair with his employees, but the inmates as well. I don't think there is a warden in the country better qualified for the job than Mr. Ragen."

The Untouchables

The prison was used in filming *The Untouchables* (1959–63). Robert Stack stars as Eliot Ness, whose elite team of incorruptible agents battled organized crime in 1930s Chicago.

Warden Frank Pate

In January 1961, Joseph Ragen was named the new director of public safety. Frank Pate, forty-six, who had been assistant to Ragen while he was warden, was named Ragen's successor as warden of the Joliet-Statesville

Warden Frank Pate awaiting the arrival of Richard Speck, May 1, 1967. *Chicago History Press.*

complex, with responsibility for some 4,200 inmates. He had begun his career as a prison guard in 1939 and climbed up through the ranks. The ambivalent relationship between punishment and rehabilitation of inmates was an issue that was close to Pate in his work in corrections. One area on which Pate focused was education. "When a man leaves the institution he has one strike against him," he said. "And, when he leaves and he's illiterate, he has two strikes against him." Inmates had the opportunity to attend school from the first grade through the junior year of college. High school diplomas were awarded under the name of Will County, Illinois. The prison had begun a two-year college program in 1957 that partnered with Wright Junior College in Chicago. Later, a third-year program was established in conjunction with Northern Illinois University. Prison officials were optimistic about the low recidivist numbers among inmates who had completed three years of college in the program.

Public criticism made Pate's job difficult. "We get a man here for a short-term sentence and they expect us to completely change him. But he's developed his attitudes from early life. The very lack of discipline in educational, moral, and religious training is what brought most of these men here."

BETTER ART SKILLS

In February 1963, a man who had drawn a three- to ten-year prison term also drew his captors in the process. It was said that twenty-five-year-old Jerry A. Wilson of Heyworth was a man who would "pen away, rather than pine away," his hours at Joliet prison. While awaiting his sentence for burglary in De Witt County and for armed robbery in McLean County, he turned out sketches by the score, cartooning sheriffs and deputies. He would be taken from De Witt to Joliet the next week. McLean County sheriff Ralph Skidmore and deputy John King were drawn by the prisoner. De Witt County officials had been targets for the Wilson pencil dozens of times, as well. Wilson was a Heyworth native who dropped out of school in his freshman year, but he said he hoped to go to school while in prison, with particular emphasis on art. "I've been drawing things since I was a kid," he said, "and I've always wanted to see something I'd drawn in print." He said that the drawings shown were hastily drawn. "I'll draw you a better one when I get to Joliet and have more time."

The Times They Are A'Changin

An outtake from October 1963 sessions for Bob Dylan's third album, *The Times They Are A'Changin'*, officially released in 1985 on the compilation *Biograph*. In the liner notes, Dylan credits Paul Clayton for the song's "beautiful melody line." The song was covered by Joan Baez in the film *Don't Look Back*. It was also on Fairport Convention's third album, *Unhalfbricking*.

"Percy's Song" by Bob Dylan:

> *Bad news, bad news; Come to me where I sleep; Turn, turn, turn again.*
> *Sayin' one of your friends is in trouble deep,*
> *Turn, turn to the rain and the wind; Tell me the trouble; Tell once to my ear,*
> *Turn, turn, turn again—Joliet prison and ninety-nine years; Turn, turn to the rain and the wind.*
> *Oh what's the charge; Of how this came to be; Turn, turn, turn again.*
> *Manslaughter in the highest of degree; Turn, turn to the rain and the wind.*
> *I sat down and wrote the best words I could write; Turn, turn, turn again.*
> *Explaining to the judge I'd be there on Wednesday night; Turn, turn to the rain.*
> *And the wind without a reply; I left by the moon; Turn, turn, turn again.*
> *And was in his chambers by the next afternoon; Turn, turn to the rain and the wind.*
> *Could ya tell me the facts? I said without fear; Turn, turn, turn again.*
> *That a friend of mine would get ninety-nine years; Turn, turn to the rain and the wind.*
> *A crash on the highway; Flew the car to a field; Turn, turn, turn again.*
> *There was four persons killed and he was at the wheel; Turn, turn to the rain and the wind.*
> *But I knew him as good as I'm knowin' myself; Turn, turn, turn again and he wouldn't harm a life*
> *That belonged to someone else; Turn, turn to the rain and the wind.*
> *The judge spoke out of the side of his mouth; Turn, turn, turn again.*

Sayin', "The witness who saw, He left little doubt;" Turn, turn to the rain and the wind.

That may be true, He's got a sentence to serve; Turn, turn, turn again.

But ninety-nine years, He just don't deserve, Turn, turn to the rain and the wind.

Too late, too late, For his case it is sealed; Turn, turn, turn again.

His sentence is passed and it cannot be repealed; Turn, turn to the rain and the wind.

But he ain't no criminal and his crime it is none; Turn, turn, turn again.

What happened to him could happen to anyone; Turn, turn to the rain and the wind.

And at that the judge jerked forward and his face it did freeze; Turn, turn, turn again.

Sayin', "Could you kindly leave, My office now, please," Turn, turn to the rain and the wind.

Well his eyes looked funny and I stood up so slow; Turn, turn, turn again.

With no other choice except for to go; Turn, turn to the rain and the wind.

I walked down the hallway and I heard his door slam; Turn, turn, turn again.

I walked down the courthouse stairs and I did not understand; Turn, turn to the rain and the wind.

And I played my guitar; Through the night to the day; Turn, turn, turn again and the only tune

My guitar could play was, "Oh the Cruel Rain and the Wind."

RICHARD HONECK

On December 20, 1963, Richard Honeck was paroled. He had spent sixty-four years of his life behind bars. When he was growing up in Hermann, Missouri, Honeck's father was a wealthy farm equipment dealer. Richard had become a telegraph operator. In 1899, when he was twenty-one years old, he stabbed to death his former school friend Walter Koeller. Honeck spent the first years of his sentence in Joliet Prison, where in 1912, he stabbed the assistant warden with a handcrafted knife. As a result, he served twenty-eight days in solitary. He was then sent to Menard. There, he worked for thirty-five years in the prison bakery. In all the years that Richard was incarcerated, he had only received a single letter—four lines from his brother in June 1904. He had two visits—one was from a

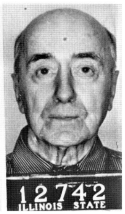

Richard Honeck was sentenced to life in prison in 1899. He was paroled on December 20, 1963. *Murderpedia.*

friend in 1904. The second visit was in 1963 from a reporter who had seen a reference to Honeck's case in the *Menard Prison Newspaper*. In the interview, Honeck told the reporter that "there must be an awful lot of traffic now, and people, compared to what I remember." After the article was published, Honeck received a mailbag of two thousand letters. He was only allowed to answer one letter per week. He said, "It'll take a long time to deal with these."

After Honeck was paroled, the reporter accompanied the old man during a car trip from Chester to St. Louis. The reporter said that his companion "was visibly amazed at the progress that had passed him by while he sat behind prison bars." Honeck said, "Why we must be going 35 miles an hour." The driver answered, "Actually, we're going 65." In St. Louis, Honeck caught a flight to San Francisco to meet his niece, Clara Orth. He remarked, "I traveled faster in that car today than I ever had in my life, and (then went) almost 10 times that fast—six miles up in the air!" Though he slowly became senile, Honeck lived on for more than a decade after his release. He died at the age of ninety-seven in an Oregon nursing home.

CATWALK REVOLT

In 1965, twenty-four-year-old rapist/robber Charles Thomas scampered up the water tower catwalk and staged a "situp," which lasted more than a week. He spent most of his days waving to guards and prisoners. He had hoarded rations in advance.

Richard Speck

Richard Speck, twenty-four, a merchant seaman and odd jobs man, was described as a drifter. He had dropped out of high school and drifted from job to job. He moved to Chicago just three weeks before breaking into a townhouse that was shared by nine nurses.

On July 14, 1966, he had been drinking since the early morning. He'd gone a few times to the Maritime Union to see about getting a job, but nothing had panned out. He drank at the Shipyard's Inn Tavern until after 10:00 p.m. He walked over a mile to a South Side townhouse where student nurses lived. He broke in late at night and repeatedly told the young women that he only wanted money and wasn't going to hurt anyone.

Speck bound the young women with strips torn from a sheet and killed eight of them during the course of several hours. Corazon Amurao, twenty-three, was a Filipino nurse who escaped death by hiding under a bed during the massacre. Speck lost count of his victims and left the apartment not knowing that Amurao was alive. She later told police that the killer had a "born to raise hell" tattoo on his arm.

Speck was found on July 17 in a skid row flophouse on Chicago's Near West Side. An emergency room surgeon at Chicago's Cook County Hospital noticed the tattoo on Speck when he was brought in after an apparent suicide attempt. He was taken to City Jail Hospital, where he suffered a seizure that was first believed to be a heart attack. Doctors later reported that Speck was suffering from pericarditis, an inflammation of the membranous sac that encases the heart.

Following a trial in Peoria, Illinois, the jury deliberated only forty-nine minutes before convicting Speck of the murders. He was sentenced on January 31, 1967, to death in the electric chair. The sentence was overturned by the U.S. Supreme Court. He was resentenced on November 21, 1972, to eight consecutive terms of 50 to 150 years for each murder, equaling 400 to 1,200 years in prison. He entered Stateville Penitentiary on June 6, 1967. He was transferred to Menard in January 1973 but returned in April, telling officials he was homesick and did not like Menard.

In September 1973, a possible conspiracy to assassinate Speck was discovered. A prisoner had just arrived from the Dupage County Jail. A new arrival first claimed he was the brother of one of Speck's eight victims but later changed his story and said he had been hired to kill Speck by another man who had been with him in the DuPage County Jail. An inmate who worked at the prison's reception and diagnostic center at Joliet Prison told the

Richard Speck arrives at Joliet Prison, May 1, 1967. *Chicago History Press.*

warden, Charles A. Felton, that the new arrival had been asking questions about Speck, including the location of his cell and his daily routine.

Richard Speck was later sent to Stateville, where he worked painting cellblocks. For years, he refused to attend parole hearings or do interviews. In 1983, he walked by two *Register Star* reporters who were touring the prison and began talking to them. He told them not to ask about his crime. "I know I didn't do right," he said. "I don't want to talk about it." He had been denied parole four times. Speck, who was then forty-one years old, would be up for consideration again in September 1984 and scoffed at the idea of getting out. He expected to die of old age in prison. "I really don't give a [expletive deleted] since my mother died. That's the only person I wanted to get out to see," he said in a rare interview in the *Rockford Register Star.* "That's the only woman I ever loved." He told the reporter that he was happy inside the prison's thirty-two-foot walls. "I'm at ease here. I love Stateville. This is my home."

He had been a problem prisoner but said he changed his ways in 1969 while he was still on death row. "My family told me if I ever hurt an employee or an inmate or tried to escape, they were through with me—I'm the outlaw of my family. That's something I can't change."

Speck died from an enlarged heart, severe emphysema and clogged arteries on December 5, 1991. He was forty-nine years old. Historians say

Guards await the arrival of Richard Speck outside the Women's Prison. *Chicago History Press.*

a certain American innocence died along with the eight student nurses in the summer of 1966. "Before July 14ᵗʰ, 1966...it was beyond our national experience that this could happen," said William Martin, Speck's chief prosecutor. "The fact that these victims didn't know the killer....The randomness of it, gave us a concern for our own safety." The Speck slayings marked the start of America's "age of mass murder," said James Alan Fox, dean of Northeastern University's College of Criminal Justice.

In May 1996, Bill Kurtis, a WBBM Channel 2 anchorman, spoke to the House Criminal Judiciary Committee about a videotape he had obtained of Richard Speck inside the Stateville Correctional Center. Kurtis had acquired the tapes from an attorney, who had previously been given them by a prison inmate. They show Speck and another man having sex, using drugs and talking about how comfortable their life was. It was hoped that lawmakers would do a thorough investigation and uncover things they have long suspected simmered beneath the surface of prison life. Lawmakers vowed to make sure current inmates did not have the same kind of freedom that Speck apparently had in 1988.

HUNGER STRIKE

On July 29, 1966, 950 prisoners went on a hunger strike. About one-fourth of the prisoners refused breakfast, one-third did not eat at noon and one-half of the inmates returned their evening meals uneaten. They were not allowed out of their cells the next day. Warden Pate said he'd received no complaints about the food. "The hot weather has been trying on nerves," said Warden Pate. "The general turmoil in the country, with disturbances in many cities, is being felt in a backlash in the prisons." The newspapers reported that the convicts' gripe was that beans were served at too many meals. Immediately after the strike ended, beans were served.

GET SMART, STARRING DON ADAMS

In a 1966 episode of *Get Smart* filmed at Joliet prison (season two, episode fourteen, "The Whole Tooth and..."). Secret Agent Maxwell Smart, played by Don Adams, deliberately gets himself arrested and sent to the prison so he can make contact with an inmate there.

RICHARD LAWSON, PRISON PHOTOGRAPHER

On April Fool's Day 1969, Richard Lawson was sentenced to prison. He was given a two- to six-year term for the possession and sale of marijuana after bringing seven ounces home from Korea when he was discharged from the army. "I didn't know anything about it except that I smoked it in the army," said Lawson. He served a year and nine months at the maximum-security Stateville Correctional Center. While there, working in a photography darkroom, he discovered a collection of long-forgotten negatives documenting life at Joliet prison from 1890 to 1930.

Lawson went on to earn a master of arts degree in cinema and photography from the University of Illinois. In 1977, Lawson told the Illinois Archives about the negatives at the prison. Stateville gave them to the archives, who lent them to Lawson to make prints. The exhibit was on display in 1981 at Southern Illinois University, where Lawson was an assistant professor.

5

JOLIET PRISON IN THE NEWS 1970-89

A BALANCE BETWEEN DISCIPLINE AND REHABILITATION

A rehabilitative program of the new state Department of Corrections resulted in a Stateville riot in June 1971, after "hard core" prisoners were removed from the general population to the old prison in Joliet. It seemed that fine-tuning was needed to find a balance between discipline and rehabilitation. Programs focusing on education, vocational training and treatment had taken shape but had mostly token implementation. The guard population had been inadequately prepared for the changes. Psychological and counseling staff were injected into the decision-making process and were unprepared to face the need for internal prison discipline.

REVEREND GORDON KNESE

Franciscan priest Reverend Gordon Knese was a chaplain in World War II in General George Patton's Third Army and since 1975 had been the Catholic chaplain for the Joliet Correctional Center in Joliet. His office was known to inmates as the "peace zone." Every day, ten to twenty inmates gathered there at noon, forgot the hostility of the institution and celebrated mass. He worked sixteen to eighteen hours a day, making daily rounds to visit the convicts, including those in the isolation cells. He died in 1987.

The chapel at the Old Joliet Prison, photographed during a tour of the prison in 2019. *Adam Kinzer Photography.*

LINCOLN PARK PIRATES

In 1973, Steve Goodman's song "Lincoln Park Pirates" was featured on the album *Someone Else's Troubles.* It is about Lincoln Towing, a company on the north side of Chicago notorious for its questionable towing practices. The song says that the tow truck drivers are "recent graduates of the charm school in Joliet."

BLACK P. STONE NATION

In April 1975, Members of the Black P. Stone Nation gang seized control of a cell block and took hostages for five hours. Word had spread through the prison grapevine that three gang members were going to be sent to Menard State Prison in southern Illinois. The inmates contended there was Ku Klux Klan activity among the guards there. All but seventy of the two hundred prisoners involved in the incident returned to their cells after tear gas was released in the area. The rest remained with hostages. One inmate was stabbed to death by other inmates after he voluntarily went to try to mediate a settlement. One of the guards said that inmates stood over them with hammers ready to beat them if state police stormed the cellblock. An inmate ordered, "If they come through the door, kill them anyway you can." The hostages were released after Warden Fred Finkbeiner broadcast a statement agreeing that the three inmates would not be transferred to Menard immediately. Seven guards and a medical technician were treated for injuries.

LARRY ANDERSON

In 1976, Larry Anderson was a seventeen-year-old running a head shop in Champaign, Illinois. A guy owed him a lot of money for dope, and he wouldn't pay. Anderson borrowed a gun and went to collect it at the restaurant where the man worked. The man gave him $2,000 at gunpoint, which made it armed robbery. "As I was leaving the gun somehow went off and knocked out the power across the street," Anderson said. "Then I tried to rip the phone off the wall but I couldn't. So I told all the waitresses to lie down, but they wouldn't. And then the guy who was driving the getaway car out front drove off without me." Anderson walked home with the money wrapped in a windbreaker, "falling out the sleeves and blowing all over." He was sentenced to six years and spent the first fourteen months at Joliet State Prison. He started writing to relieve the boredom of prison life. He met a CBS cameraman who spotted his writing while filming in Joliet. He submitted scripts to *Saturday Night Live* and WKRP in Cincinnati, sold one-liners to Joan Rivers and worked on a screenplay with Cheech and Chong. He hoped to go to California in November 1980.

Deadlock

In February 1977, Governor James R. Thompson addressed concerns of overcrowding and violence at the state prisons. The transfer of a substantial number of inmates to other facilities offered hope to a tense situation. A riot in July 1977 at Pontiac Correctional Center left three guards dead. As a result, Pontiac, Stateville and Joliet Prisons were all put on deadlock, which prohibited inmates from leaving their cells. By October 7, only Joliet had been taken off.

From November 3 through 5, 1977, guards at Stateville and Joliet Prisons staged a wildcat walkout to protest prison politics and discrimination. A report said that guards and prisoners had to live and work in dirty and "inhuman" conditions. Uninterrupted eight-hour guard duty in unlighted towers—some of them without toilets—had dulled the abilities of correctional officers to respond to emergencies. Guards were punished unfairly. The report criticized recruitment and training procedures and said that affirmative action programs were faulty.

John Wayne Gacy

In 1968, John Wayne Gacy was convicted and sentenced to serve ten years in the Iowa State Reformatory. He was released in 1970, after serving only eighteen months. A condition of his parole was that he would relocate to Chicago to live with his mother. In between 1972 and 1978, when he should have still been in prison in Iowa, he raped, tortured and murdered at least thirty-three teenage boys and young men.

He was sentenced to death. He was transferred under heavy guard to Joliet Reception and Classification Center in March 1980. After a battery of exams, he was driven to Menard Correctional Center. He was the first inmate at that facility's death row cell block unit. He remained incarcerated on death row for fourteen years. When Gacy's final appeal was denied, he was transferred to Stateville. The "killer clown" was escorted to the execution chamber to receive a lethal injection on May 10, 1994.

Gacy's last formal statement was that "taking his life would not compensate for the loss of the others and that this was the state murdering him." Corrections Department spokesman Nic Howell said that Gacy had told him earlier in the day that his last words were going to be "kiss my ass." In 2019, an episode of the Travel Channel's *Ghost Adventures* was filmed at Joliet Prison for an episode called "Serial Killer Spirits: John Gacy Prison."

John Wayne Gacy hides his face as he is led through the Des Plaines police station on December 22, 1978. *Michael Budrys*, Chicago Tribune.

THE BLUES BROTHERS

John Belushi's character "Joliet Jake Blues" is in Joliet Correctional Center at the beginning of the John Landis film *The Blues Brothers* (1980). His brother Elwood Blues (Dan Aykroyd) picks him up in front of the prison when he's released. The film also features John Candy, Ray Charles, Aretha Franklin, Cab Calloway, Chaka Khan, James Brown, Carrie Fisher, Twiggy, Steven Spielberg, John Walsh and Henry Gibson.

Brothers Jake and Elwood were first a musical comedy skit on *Saturday Night Live*. They later released an album of old blues jazz songs called *Briefcase Full of Blues*. It was recorded in the summer of 1978, when the Blues Brothers opened for Steve Martin during his nine-day, sold-out stand at the Universal Amphitheater. The number-one record sold over two million copies. (The names Belushi and Aykroyd did not appear on the album, as the comedians stayed in character. Belushi and Aykroyd only did interviews about the Blues Brothers projects if they were done in character.)

Above: Joliet Jake.
Promotional photo from
The Blues Brothers,
1980.

Left: The Blues
Brothers perform
at Chicagofest on
August 3, 1979. *Don
Bierman for* Chicago
Sun-Times, *Chicago
History Press.*

The second album would be the soundtrack to the promised Blues Brothers movie, which would be based on the liner notes from the first album—the fictional story of two brothers who spent their childhood in the basement of the St. Helen of the Blessed Shroud orphanage, hanging out with a Black janitor and learning the blues. Elwood picks up Jake when he's released from Joliet Prison. Soon they are on a "mission from God" to raise money to save the struggling orphanage. "Along the way they alienate the American Nazi Party, the Illinois State Police, the Cook County Sheriff's Department, the Chicago Police and this woman played by Carrie Fisher who continually tries to kill them," said director John Landis. Sean Daniel, vice president of production at Universal, said that it would be "a road-picture musical like no one's ever seen before."

On Thursdays, [Joliet] *serve*[s] *a wicked pepper steak.*

Chase scenes were filmed on most of Chicago's expressways and thoroughfares, including Lake Shore Drive. The Universal Pictures production filmed ten weeks of its planned fourteen-week shooting schedule in Chicago, Joliet, the suburbs and downstate. Filming began on August 13, 1979, and strict secrecy was demanded. Universal wanted to avoid crowds and pre-publicity. Reporters and cameras were not allowed on set. A few pictures surfaced, but all were taken of the outdoor filming and most with telephoto lenses from one hundred yards or more away. Extras—south suburban kids, housewives and retired guys—made thirty-five to fifty dollars for the day. More than 100 old squad cars were purchased from the Chicago Police Department. The movie set a world record for wrecked cars—103 automobiles were destroyed during the shooting. Twelve Bluesmobiles were built for the film—one designed specifically to be destroyed. The movie was estimated to profit $20 million in revenue for the State of Illinois.

In a June 1980 interview, director John Landis told the backstory of the Blues Brothers.

While John [Belushi] *was making* Animal House *in Oregon, he made friends with a fella* [Curtis Salgado of the Robert Cray Blues Band] *who is a real blues maniac. He became a real authority on it and when he got back to New York, he and Danny, who shares a passion for black American music, sat around talking and they invented these characters—Joliet Jake and Elwood Blues. It had nothing to do with* Saturday Night Live. *Then they used to warm up the audience*

135

and one night they said, "Well, let's go on the air." But long before that we had talked about a movie and the movie was a reality long before the record. They just figured for fun they'd go open for Steve Martin at the Amphitheater [in Los Angeles] *and a record was made of it. No one, and I mean no one expected that.*

He went on to describe the challenges of filming the movie: "This movie is large. Huge. I mean, there are dance scenes involving 600 people. There's a car chase around Chicago to Daley Plaza that involves hundreds of people and colossal stunts. That's one of the reasons we've kept it essentially a secret. I mean nobody knows anything about this picture. And, I mean, it's a true epic. There are scenes with 15,000 people. Wait till you see what we did in Cook Plaza!"

Reviewer Steve Hall wrote that the fast-moving musical comedy would delight most audiences. He highlighted the musical numbers—the Triple Rock Baptist Church scene, featuring James Brown; the sizzling Aretha Franklin song "Think"; John Lee Hooker performing "Boom Boom" in the streets of Chicago; and the unforgettable Ray Charles demonstrating on a "worn-out" keyboard at Ray's Music exchange. But he pointed out that the movie had one major fault: "The audience is asked to believe that everyone wearing some sort of uniform in Illinois [police, firemen and soldiers] would take part in a gigantic all-night chase to catch two seedy hoods who have done nothing more than violate traffic laws."

The Old Joliet Prison planned to host a two-day party celebrating the fortieth anniversary of the movie on August 21 and 22, 2020. Unfortunately, the event had to be canceled due to COVID-19 restrictions. It is hoped that this event will still be held at a later date. The plans include a showing of the movie, Blues Brothers replica bands and a re-creation of the country music stage where Jake and Elwood were protected by chicken wire while singing blues to an unappreciative audience. The event will double as a fundraiser for the prison restoration project. Promoters are hoping to get Dan Aykroyd to put in an appearance.

JAMES PANGBURN

On April 28, 1981, James Pangburn, twenty-one, hanged himself after a week at Joliet. He had repeatedly been the victim of sexual assault by other inmates. An autopsy revealed that he had swallowed two notes indicating that a Chicago street gang, the Disciples, had gotten keys to his cell and were able to enter at will. He blamed guards for not protecting him. His family sued the State of Illinois.

He Went to the Bar

In May 1984, inmates were working at a car wash near the prison. A guard noticed one of them was missing. A search turned him up at a local bar, where he'd sat down to have a beer without any money. The inmate was happy to see the guard, since he had no plan for payment. He was returned to the prison within three hours of his escape. The inmate, who was close to parole time, had six years added to his time for the escape.

Three Attempts to Escape

In September 1984, inmates working in the yard discovered an inmate attempting to escape over the wall. Not wanting to lose their privileges, the inmates dragged him to the office. Francis Scott had been housed in the North Segregation Unit. Deep Lock was supposed to be impossible to escape. He was escorted to the legal library that day, where he had obtained a piece of a hacksaw blade. Hiding the blade in his hair, he got back to his cell without it being discovered. He sawed out two bars, which made a hole of sixteen inches by six inches. He took off all his clothing, wet himself down with soap and water and slipped through the hole in the bars. He overpowered the officer at the desk and took his clothing, tying the officer up in a closet. He left the unit and walked to the north wall, where he was found by the other inmates.

However, guards were unable to recover the hacksaw blade, and two weeks later, Scott escaped again. This time, he went east to Sally Port no. 2. At the top of the port, he was only about ten feet from the top of the wall. He kept jumping but could not get high enough. He was brought down and returned to a cell—this time in Menard Correctional Center.

In June 1986, he was brough back to Will County Courthouse to be tried on the escape attempts. When he arrived, Scott told the officers that his legs were numb from the leg irons and asked that they be removed. When the officer unshackled him, he bolted. Since the inmate had kept his hands behind his back, they hadn't realized he'd been able to get out of the handcuffs during the drive. The new Will County Jail was under construction, and the construction workers took him down before he was able to get away.

OVERKILL

In May 1986, there was a fight in the dining room of Joliet Prison. The inmates ignored orders to stop, and the officer in the tower fired rounds into the ceiling. They still did not stop, so the officer pointed the gun at the inmates and pulled the trigger. The problem is, she didn't stop. Six inmates were shot. None were seriously harmed, but the shooter was badly shaken up. She was transferred to another institution. But for quite a while, inmates would look up to check if a woman was in the tower when they went to supper. They would think twice about starting any trouble.

AN ESCAPE OUT OF THE MOVIES

In 1987, inmate Donald escaped from Stateville by blending in with a movie crew that was there filming the movie *Weeds*, starring Nick Nolte. Donald was arrested three weeks later in North Dakota and brought back to the North Segregation Unit at Joliet Prison. He often called for the nurse and complained of all sorts of ailments. He finally got an appointment for an examination at an outside hospital. When he was leaving for the appointment, a thorough search was done, and he was found to have a homemade piece of contraband fashioned to look like a pistol taped to the inside of his leg. He planned to grab a nurse and demand that the officers hand over their guns and then he would have a real gun and escape.

6
JOLIET PRISON IN THE NEWS 1990-2020

THE WRONG SIDE OF THE LAW

On February 15, 1990, a thirteen-year guard at the Joliet Correctional Center was arrested and charged with aiding the escape of six inmates from the maximum-security prison. William Smith, forty-six, of Joliet, was accused of smuggling in hacksaw blades that were used to cut cell bars in the units where the inmates were held. The six inmates apparently escaped in groups of twos, with one group sawing through the cell bars and passing the hacksaw blades along to the next pair. The inmates' absence went unnoticed during at least five routine checks between 11:00 p.m. Saturday and 7:00 a.m. Sunday. Two of the inmates actually hailed a cab outside the prison walls after the break. The cab driver didn't notice their uniforms because the convicted killers wore winter coats. They moved into an abandoned gymnasium on the South Side but ventured out in search of cocaine and were arrested during a raid at a home in the area. Another of the inmates, Tommy Munoz, twenty-two, was recaptured on Sunday. Terry Colburn, twenty-one, who was serving a five-year-sentence for burglary, was arrested at a Calumet Park towing company while waiting for a truck ride to his home in Mississippi. A fifth man was talked into turning himself in by his parents after he'd returned home to Wyoming, Illinois. Twenty-one-year-old David Rodriguez of Chicago, serving a twenty-five-year term for murder, remained at large.

HOLLYWOOD

A riot scene from *Natural Born Killers* (1994), starring Woody Harrelson and Juliet Lewis, was filmed in the one-time women's prison across the street. In 1994, *Saturday Night Live* did a skit concerning prison life with Chris Farley and Martin Lawrence that mentioned Joliet. In 1999, Kevin Bacon filmed *Stir of Echoes* there. The Columbia TriStar show *Early Edition*, season three episode thirteen, "The Last Untouchable," features a fictional mobster, Antonio Birelli, played by Ernest Borgnine, being released from the prison.

In 2003, Governor Rod Blagojevich signed production rebates into law. "Illinois film production rebounded to $77 million in 2004. In the first half of 2005, Hollywood dropped $68 million into the state economy."

In 2005, Jennifer Aniston and Clive Owen filmed *Derailed*. In the movie, two business executives having an affair are blackmailed by a violent criminal, and the two must turn the tables on him to save their families. Also in 2005, the television series *My Fair Brady*, starring Christopher Knight from the *Brady Bunch*, was filmed. Some characters in *Saw II* (2005) are ex-Joliet inmates.

Dax Shepard and Will Arnett starred in *Let's Go to Prison* in 2006.

The prison was also used as the location of Fox River for the first season of Fox Network's *Prison Break* television show. In the show, an innocent man is sent to death row. His only hope is his brother, who gets himself into the same prison in order to break them both out. Wentworth Miller, who stars as Michael Scofield, said the prison helped a great deal in keeping him grounded in the character. "When you're surrounded by 3-foot-thick walls, you really understand how impossible his task is." The show used the former prison for early shooting in the infirmary, the chapel, some of the sheds, solitary confinement and the yard. "Producer Garry Brown said the show's creators searched the country for a prison—and were wowed to find one that was vacant, open for shooting and featuring such beautiful-yet-foreboding Victorian architecture....Little was needed to transform the site—except adding more dirt and grime." Amaury Nolasco, who plays Scofield's cellmate, said he often passed cells and wondered about the men who occupied them and their ultimate fates. "The minute you walk in you feel this energy and this cloud of all the spirits that are probably going by," Nolasco said. "The prison is a character in itself. It's there. You have to acknowledge it. It's an ensemble cast—including the prison."

In 2007, the Fox Network show *Bones*, season two episode twelve, "The Man in the Cell," features Joliet as the prison where serial killer Howard Epps is held. It is known as Bay View Federal Penitentiary on the show.

Johnny Depp and Christian Bale filmed *Public Enemies* (2009) at Joliet. The action thriller is about Depression-era bank robber John Dillinger.

Joliet Prison was briefly featured in *Flash*, season two "Family of Rogues" (2015), as Iron Heights prison. In season one, episode nine of Netflix's *Mindhunter*, Joliet is shown as the prison holding serial killer Richard Speck. A scene of the hit show *Empire* was filmed in front of the administration building.

CONGRESSMAN MEL REYNOLDS

In 1995, former congressman Mel Reynolds was admitted to Joliet, to serve a five-year sentence for sexual misconduct and obstruction of justice. Within forty-eight hours, he was taken to a minimum-security prison in downstate Vienna. He was considered a security risk at Joliet, due to his anti-gang stances.

JOLIET PRISON ORDERED CLOSED

In 2001, Governor George Ryan was looking to cut the state budget. Joliet's increasingly dire shortfall of its annual $4 million budget definitely stood out as a possible target. For decades, it had served mainly as the state prison system's intake valve. Most prisoners stayed about ten days and were processed and then sent to another prison. Only about two hundred maximum-security inmates were serving long sentences at the Collins Street facility.

Despite many voices raised in opposition, Ryan felt there was little choice. He ordered the complete closure of Joliet Correctional Center. Warden Ron Matrisciano said, "As a prison, I really believe Joliet has always been the crown jewel of this department….Joliet is synonymous with the penal system." On February 16, 2002, the last of the long-term prisoners were transferred. Many of Joliet's five hundred employees were transferred to Stateville and other prisons, though they weren't happy about it. "It's like breaking up a family," they said.

> *One of the toughest places a man could do time has become a victim of it.*
> —*Don Babwin*

Prison wire, taken on a tour of the prison in 2019. *Adam Kinzer Photography.*

One prisoner, Phil LaPointe, also didn't like the idea of the prison closing. He was convicted of murder in the late 1970s and had spent most of his seventeen years behind bars at Joliet. When interviewed by Don Babwin, he said, "No, I don't want to go. The smaller population here is conducive to a more friendly [relationship] between inmates and staff. They treat you like an individual."

Ben McCreadie was at Joliet Correctional Center for more than twelve years. He was convicted of murdering state conservation police officer Dave Bowers in 1990 after getting caught in a love triangle with Bowers's wife. A musician who plays trumpet, trombone and harmonica, his prized possession was an Israeli-made pear wood recorder. During a general crackdown, guards took it in 1998. He turned to painting, but they chopped the handles off and gave him the brushes on nubs. So, he planted perennials in the prison gardens and became known as the flower guy. He was among the last prisoners shipped out when the old prison closed on February 16, 2002.

McCreadie told reporter Lou Carlozo that he was dreading the long bus ride to Menard. "That's an eight-hour bus ride on a seat like this," he knocked hard on his plastic chair. "They've got the windows blocked so you can't see anything. To me, it's like an eight-hour elevator ride. I hope I don't get sick," he said. "I haven't been in a vehicle for over a decade."

Due to the obsolete and dangerous nature of the old buildings, a new facility was being built at Stateville to handle intake and processing. The $90 million state-of-the-art inmate reception center at Stateville Prison would replace the current reception center that was being operated at the aging Joliet Correctional Center. The intake center continued to operate, processing inmates who were new to the State of Illinois penal system, until March 2004. Finally, the doors closed for the last time, and the remaining staff began a new chapter at the new Stateville processing facility. Shortly after Joliet Prison closed, the federal government looked at buying the property, but a deal was never made. The city assessed the 180-acre property with the hope of redeveloping it.

The City of Joliet waged a losing battle to block the state from housing its worst sex offenders in an annex of the prison. "The annex housed more than 200 convicted sex offenders who had completed their prison terms but were committed to a treatment and detention center after being deemed too dangerous to release. They were technically patients, not prisoners, but city leaders didn't see it that way." On August 7, 2006, they were moved to downstate Rushville.

WHORES AND THIEVES OF THE WORST KIND

In 2003, Mara Dodge's book *Whores and Thieves of the Worst Kind: A Study of Women, Crime and Prisons 1835–2000* was released. A historian at Westfield State College in Massachusetts, Dodge lived in Chicago from 1982 to 1997. Working on her PhD at the University of Illinois, she began this book as her dissertation. She realized there were only two books written on the history of women in prison. Working at Stateville, Dwight Correctional Center and Joliet Correctional Center, she had access to the records. She spent time in basements, looking through files, and looking at microfilm.

JOLIET PRISONS: IMAGES IN TIME, A PICTORIAL HISTORY

The same year, semiretired Joliet Junior College history professor Robert Sterling published *Joliet Prisons: Images in Time, a Pictorial History*. It is a look at how Joliet's famous prisons got their start. From the Bertillon System to baking bread for the Great Chicago Fire, this book documents how prison culture changed over time.

Prison Park Opens

In July 2009, Joliet opened Prison Park with kiosks of information about the history of the prison just outside the walls. In 2011, the Chicago Metropolitan Agency for planning awarded Joliet free consulting and planning assistance to study the prison project. The Chicago-based Urban Land Institute also provided assistance.

Tough

In 2010, Donald "Duke" Cartwright wrote *Tough: An Insider's View of the World's Toughest Profession* about his years as a guard at Joliet and Stateville. He said, "This book is dedicated to my family, who stood behind me during the 33 years of my being gone to work on most Holidays and other festivities of the family. This is further dedicated to all the hardworking prison guards, working a thankless, but very necessary job for society. I salute all those who have passed on to their final reward, and a heart-felt prayer for those still in the struggle."

Vandals

On July 25, 2013, at approximately 3:15 a.m. a fire appeared to have started inside the walls of Joliet Correctional Center and was contained to the warehouse. The fire smoldered until around 7:30 a.m., when firemen soaked the warehouse from extension ladders.

Though the gates to the prison had been welded shut, there were reports that people had been trying to get inside. The building had not had electrical or plumbing service in years. Joliet Fire Department chief Ray Randich told ABC Chicago that in twenty-eight years it was the "first time I've had to break into a prison." The prison has continued to be the target of vandals and trespassers. A stone lion that stood outside the women's building across the street was stolen.

Tours of the Prison

In 2018, the Joliet Area Historical Museum began running tours of the penitentiary for Route 66 travelers. It offers a one-and-a-half-hour walking

The administration building, photographed on a tour of the prison in 2019. *Courtesy Adam Kinzer Photography.*

historical tour, which covers the general history of the prison from 1858 to the present. The haunted history tour covers the darker stories of the historical prison as you walk through the prison at dusk. The guard tour is led by two docents who worked at the prison while it was still in operation. They tell of daily life at the prison during their time there—a more personal take on the site's history. The photography tour is a four-hour tour of the expansive historic prison site, taking photos in the morning light with supervised access to the prison yard and predesignated buildings. Tickets can be purchased online at jolietprison.org.

Chicago Hauntings

In October and November 2018, the Joliet Area Historical Museum partnered with Chicago Hauntings to offer paranormal tours and ghost hunts at the Old Joliet Prison. Chicago Hauntings staff was featured on SYFY, A&E, PBS, Travel Channel, Destination America, TLC and Maury Povich. Tickets can be purchased online at chicagohauntings.com.

Blooze Brothers mobile at the Prison Break-In of 2018. *Joliet Area Historical Museum, Illinois.*

THE GREAT JOLIET PRISON BREAK-IN

In 2018, more than three thousand people attended the first Great Joliet Prison Break-In, hosted by the Joliet Area Historical Museum. The following year, on August 24, Chicago's Ides of March Band, Hot Mess, Great Moments in Vinyl and the Nikki Hill Band played at the second annual event. All proceeds from the fundraiser were to benefit efforts to secure, stabilize and showcase the Old Joliet Prison.

ART FROM THE ASHES

Art from the Ashes was a special exhibition of the Old Joliet Prison Burnt District Artists that ran from February 1 through September 30, 2019. It showcased the work of a group of Joliet-based artists assembled in 2018. The group formed in response to a challenge to repurpose items destroyed during the four acts of arson at the prison site between 2013 and 2017. There were also various educational companion programs hosted by the museum, including demonstrations, discussions and presentations by some of the local artists whose works were included in the exhibit.

GHOST ADVENTURES

The Ghost Adventures team came to explore the grounds of the Old Joliet Prison. It filmed an episode that focused on a cell briefly occupied by John Wayne Gacy as part of a serial killer spirits miniseries slated to air on the Travel Channel on October 12, 2019.

DRINK IN THE CLINK CRAFT BEER FESTIVAL

Drink in the Clink is a two-hundred-plus craft beer festival to benefit the further restoration and enhancement of the Old Joliet Prison. Whether you are a craft beer aficionado or you just like beer, it's a chance to not only enjoy some amazing beverages but also step onto the prison yard and see some of the buildings at Old Joliet Prison. This includes walking through the same gate that Joliet Jake walked out in the *Blues Brothers*.

FALL FLICKS IN THE YARD

An October 23 and 24, 2020 fundraiser event had to be canceled due to State of Illinois COVID-19 restrictions. State of Illinois Heightened Mitigation Strategies for Region 7 limited indoor and outdoor gatherings to under twenty-five persons.

RESTORING THE OLD PRISON

A message in the tile floor of a cell block in the old Joliet Prison once spoke to the men imprisoned there. Now it represents the efforts to restore the prison:

It's Never too Late to Mend.

A section of the tile floor of the prison hospital reads "It's Never Too Late to Mend." *Adam Kinzer Photography.*

BIBLIOGRAPHY

Armstrong, J.T. "Warden of State Prison Has Plan to Stop Unrest." *Dispatch* (Moline, IL), April 28, 1930.

Babwin, Don. "Governor's Call: Time's Up for Notorious Joliet Prison." *Cincinnati Enquirer*, December 19, 2001.

———. "Joliet Prison Closing after More Than 140 Years." *Daily Republican Register* (Mount Carmel, IL), December 17, 2001.

Bailey, Tom. "Sex Slayer Executed at Joliet." *Marshall (MI) Evening Chronicle*, October 15, 1935.

Burghart, Tara. "Joliet Prison a Star on 'Prison Break.'" *Sentinel* (Carlisle, PA), November 12, 2005.

Carlozo, Lou. "Prison Blues." *Chicago Tribune*. February 18, 2002.

Cipriani, E.M. "Treatment of Inmates Alleged Responsible for Riots at Joliet." *Dispatch* (Moline, IL), March 19, 1931.

Dardick, Hal. "Don't Call It Prison Town." *Chicago Tribune*, August 13, 2006.

Dash, Mike. "The Longest Prison Sentences Ever Served." *A Blast from the Past* (blog), July, 24 2010. Mikedashhistory.com.

Dodge, L. Mara. *Whores and Thieves of the Worst Kind: A Study of Women, Crime, and Prisons, 1885–2000*. DeKalb: Northern Illinois University Press, 2006.

Dwyer, Orville. "Midget: The Ultra Modern Bandit and Crook." *Sunday News* (Lancaster, PA), July 17, 1927.

Early, L.E. "Death Beckons one of the Brainiest Men in Country Because He's a Criminal." *Evening News* (Wilkes-Barr, PA), July 18, 1927.

———. "Gunning for Money Becomes Feminine Game in Lake City." *Decatur (AL) Daily*, May 3, 1927.

Fusaro, David. "I Was a 'Blues Brothers' Extra." *Southtown Star* (Tinley Park, IL), September 23, 1979.

Gowran, Clay. "Crime Expert Calls for End of Jury Trials." *Chicago Tribune*, April 30, 1955.

Hall, Steve. "Blues Revue Brews Stardom for 'Brothers.'" *Indianapolis News*, June 24, 1980.

Hoffman, Gene. "New Effort at Joliet Prison Break Foiled." *Republican-Northwestern* (Belvidere IL), May 13, 1927.

Knoedelseder, William K. Jr. "The Blues Brothers—'Saturday Night' Jive. *Los Angeles Times*, February 18, 1979.

Lane, Charles. "Heartbreak Hotel." *Chicago Magazine*, August 2006. https://www.chicagomag.com,

Logan, Joe. "Oh, Brothers! California Scheming in Shooting the Blues." *Minneapolis Star*, June 20, 1980.

Okon, Bob. "Converting Collins Street." *Herald News* (Joliet, IL), September 15, 2015.

Renshaw, Charles, Jr. "Chaplain Courageous." *San Francisco Examiner*, January 16, 1949.

Ryan, Maureen. "Joliet: Hollywood's New Favorite." *Chicago Tribune*, August 25, 2005.

Swislow, William. "Art from Inside." *Chicago Tribune*, November 8, 1992.

Tremeear, Janice. *Illinois Haunted Route 66*. Charleston, SC: The History Press, 2013.

Wilson, Tom. "One-Cent Coin Good Luck for Prison Head." *Register Mail* (Galesburg, IL), November 9, 2010.

INDEX

ABOUT THE AUTHOR

lso the author of *Old Joliet Prison: When Convicts Wore Stripes*, Amy has spent the last twenty-five years as a teacher and a genealogist. Many of her years teaching were spent working in juvenile justice. She earned a master's degree in history from Illinois State University. She loves to travel and is always planning the next adventure. Her greatest joy is her family—her husband, Jay, and their four children, who have grown up to be amazing adults.

Visit us at
www.historypress.com